WHAT PEOPLE ARE SAYING ABOUT

PAGAN PORTALS – CELTIC WITCHCRAFT

As a witch who adores ancient Irish mythology, I love this book by Mabh Savage. *Pagan Portals – Celtic Witchcraft* offers a fascinating glimpse into the magic of nature, the gods and goddesses, and the beliefs of the past. It shows how we can adapt the wisdom of the Celts to practise witchcraft in the modern world. It is well researched, beautifully written and highly inspiring.
Lucya Starza, author of A Bad Witch's Blog

A clear and informative introduction for the Celtic witch. Wisdom shines through on every page to encourage and lead the reader down a magical path firmly grounded in practical experience.

Beautifully written to inspire anyone who resonates with the Celtic tradition to delve deeper into the craft and understand its magic on every level.
Sheena Cundy, author of *The Madness and the Magic*, Moon Books

Mabh Savage's Pagan *Portals – Celtic Witchcraft* is an inspired look at how to incorporate older Celtic beliefs into modern witchcraft practice. This short text deftly weaves together personal experience, myth, magic, and actual practice into a seamless whole that resonates with poetry and spirit. A truly unique look at how the old ways and folk beliefs can and do exist today in the hearts of modern witches just as powerfully as they always have.
Morgan Daimler, author of *Fairy Witchcraft* and *Pagan Portals – The Morrigan,* Moon Books

A beautifully written book looking into the myths and legends that support the modern day practice of Celtic Witchcraft drawing on Mabh's personal experiences of walking this pathway and the wisdom of the Tuatha De Danann.

Rachel Patterson, author of *Grimoire of a Kitchen Witch,* Moon Books

Pagan Portals
Celtic Witchcraft

Modern Witchcraft meets Celtic Ways

Pagan Portals

Celtic Witchcraft

Modern Witchcraft meets Celtic Ways

Mabh Savage

Winchester, UK
Washington, USA

First published by Moon Books, 2016
Moon Books is an imprint of John Hunt Publishing Ltd., Laurel House, Station Approach,
Alresford, Hants, SO24 9JH, UK
office1@jhpbooks.net
www.johnhuntpublishing.com
www.moon-books.net

For distributor details and how to order please visit the 'Ordering' section on our website.

ISBN: 978 1 78535 314 7
Library of Congress Control Number: 2015952169

A CIP catalogue record for this book is available from the British Library.

Design: Stuart Davies

Printed and bound by CPI Group (UK) Ltd, Croydon, CR0 4YY, UK

We operate a distinctive and ethical publishing philosophy in all
areas of our business, from our global network of authors to
production and worldwide distribution.

CONTENTS

Dedicated to Emma, for believing in me; and in fairies.

Introduction and Acknowledgements

I started writing this book in the hope that my experiences might help others find a foothold on a magical path. I was born into a world of mystery, a lucky child of parents who lived lives of seasonal sorcery. I know not everyone is lucky enough to find their inner spark so early in life though, and this book is for anyone looking to bring some magic into their lives.

The Celts are a fascinating, mysterious and oddly diverse race of people. They had gods that walked the earth as mortal and immortal heroes, and strange creatures from other realms. I mostly reach out to my own Irish ancestors, but the Celts spread themselves far and wide across the world, so the chances are most of us have some Celtic ancestry deep within our genome. Even if not, the inspiration and wonder that the Celtic legends bring has universal appeal. To be inspired by the Celts is as powerful a motivator as to be descended from them, and with witchcraft, motivation and intention is everything.

Everyone walks their own path, but that doesn't mean they have to walk alone. Witchcraft is about power that comes from within, and those who wield that power do have a tendency to attract others of the same ilk.

I have been lucky enough to cross paths with people of varying religions and beliefs, who have been wise, kind and patient enough to let me pick their brains and work with them; sometimes in ritual, sometimes in practical magic and sometimes in everyday hard graft.

Whatever kind of witch you decide to be, never take the people around you for granted, and always be thankful for the smallest kindness.

This book introduces you to one way of making magic; a natural way, influenced by the remnants of Celtic culture and lore that we know of. If something in this book inspires you to find your own path, then I have been successful. If you are already walking your own path, you may find in these pages a fresh perspective; a new connection to the world.

Thank you to all those who have stepped in time beside me on my path; my fellow witches, priests and priestesses, magicians and custodians of nature. To them, and to you, dear reader, I say this: may your own path rise smoothly to meet your feet.

Chapter One

A Witch on a Celtic Path

Celtic Triad: Three things to be avoided by the Wise: expecting the impossible, grieving over the irretrievable, fearing the inevitable.

Witchcraft is often described as a new age religion, especially with the emergence of Wicca, the religious practice strongly associated with modern witchcraft, in the 20th century. However, you only need to look as far as the nearest fairy tale anthology to realise the term 'witch' has been with us for millennia, in many different forms. The Old English words wicce and wicca were used for female and male magical practitioners as far back as 890 CE. This shows us that witchcraft is extremely 'old age' indeed! Throughout the generations the term witch has moved from meaning wise person (usually a woman) to feared crone or hilarious hermit. As with all things that are not understood by the majority, respect gives way to fear, and fear to anger and ridicule, and as we have seen through the centuries, hatred and murder.

Reassuringly, at least one ancient culture has inspired multiple stories of prophets, prophetesses, druids, poets, bards, satirists, shape-shifters, gods, goddesses and more who are not only respected but accepted as a part of day-to-day life. I'm speaking of the Celts, who adored and accepted what we now refer to as the supernatural. They accepted that gods and goddesses walked among us, and that animals held spirits and voices of their own. They knew of the power of trees, and the binding ways of words. They were held by geas, or taboo, which could not be broken. They made heroes of warriors and the wise alike. They believed in sacred objects, and great quests to find such. They stood face to face and toe to toe with the fae, those unearthly being from under the hills or beyond a spiritual veil.

It is no wonder then, that modern day Paganism retains so much of their influence. This includes, as you probably know, festival dates, deities and places of worship or respect. The biggest example is the Wheel of the Year, the seasonal structure for many Pagan paths. This is based on the festivals we believe the Celts celebrated, the four primary ones being Imbolc (or Imbolg), Beltane (or Beltain), Lughnasadh (not Lammas; Lammas is an Anglo Saxon celebration although probably has similar roots – who doesn't want to celebrate at the height of summer!) and Samhain.

The Celts seem to have regarded Samhain as the boundary between the light and dark parts of the year; summer's death and winter's rebirth. It's no surprise then, that many Pagans and witches see this as the start of the new year. Robert Graves famously used the Holly King and the Oak King to represent summer and winter, locked in an eternal struggle for power (*The White Goddess*, 1978), which is an image that seems clearly inspired by the Celtic way of dividing light and dark, and of course, their reverence for trees. Many Wiccans or people on a similar path will find this metaphor familiar, as it is a core part of the Wheel of the Year now for some; a way to visualise the sun reaching its peak at midsummer, and the triumph of the dark in midwinter.

So why, when we can all see that most 'Neopaganism' has such Celtic roots anyway, am I a Celtic witch? What does that mean, and how is it different from any other type of witchcraft?

Well let's look at the 'witch' part first; when I say I am a witch, I'm saying I harness the energies around and within me to instigate change. Mahatma Ghandi said: 'Be the change we wish to see in the world.'

Much of witchcraft is this; using our inherent power as a sentient being to be a force for transformation. Anyone can do this with training, and the will and patience to gain a deeper understanding of the universe around them. You don't need to be religious, although many witches do follow a religious path, such as Wicca or another polytheistic faith. For me, witchcraft is more about having faith in yourself and your own skill, although I also accept the existence of other-worldly beings and forces.

On to the Celtic part: I am deeply influenced by my Celtic ancestry, and walk a path side by side with the Tuatha Dé Danann; the great folk who were one of the many races that invaded Ireland. *Lebor Gabála Érenn*, the *Book of the Taking of Ireland*, is an 11th century text describing eight periods throughout Ireland's 'history' (the book's contents are of more mythological interest rather than indisputable fact) including the rise and fall of the Tuatha Dé Danann. The text tells us that they came to Ireland on dark clouds, and that they viewed their men of arts as gods, and knew the incantations of druids. It is sung in the text that they are 'without a covenant of religion'; indeed it seems that while they accept the reality of larger-than-life heroes and magical transformation, they revere none as being above or beyond them. Everything is worldly and everything is within reach. This is why I feel my craft belongs to a Celtic source more than any other. I am stubborn to the point of foot stamping and petulance, yet patient enough to wait longer than most would in a tense situation. I will fight when necessary and be quiet when not. I know when presentation is important, and when subtlety is key. I accept that part of me is divine, and acknowledge that divinity within others, but I am not cowed by it. I know when to use my craft, and when elbow grease and hard work will give me a better result.

The Celts took pride in taking a skill and honing it to perfection, but also mastering a number of other skills along the way. They revered wisdom as much as physical strength, which is something that I often find lacking in our modern world. The Irish Celts in particular had strict social customs and manners, and because barely anything was written down, words had a unique power that is difficult to recreate in an age where there is a record of everything.

Of course the Celts were not solely Irish, in fact it is now thought by modern historians that the Celts were various tribes who moved across Europe during the Iron Age, perhaps even from the far east, travelling through the Mediterranean, the Germanic and Baltic countries, and possibly as far north as Scandinavia. Because of the aforementioned lack of Celtic literature, their tales and myths come to us via word of mouth and the work of Christian scholars such as Áed Ua Crimthainn, compiler of the *Book of Leinster*. In the British Isles the stories that cling closest to our hearts tend to be the Welsh and the Irish, particularly the *Mabinogion* and the *Ulster Cycle*. My heart lies with my Irish ancestry, mainly because I have been moved and inspired all my life by the tales of the *Ulster Cycle*, and because bizarre twists and turns along my path have brought me into contact with others fascinated with our Celtic heritage. So, while I speak of the Tuatha Dé Danann and their influence on my life, you may find a stronger connection with Gaulish deities, or perhaps the Welsh. Use my experience to create a bond that is unique to you.

'But I don't have any Celtic ancestors,' you may say. Well, I believe you absolutely can follow a Celtic path without any known Celtic ancestry. Our entire world would be a different place today if the Celts had not existed, so all of us can say our existence has been in some way influenced by the Celts. Celtic names, tales and art pop up throughout modern popular culture, from films to video games. The famous Halo gaming franchise has a screeching vehicle called a banshee, based on the mythical creature who wailed to foretell death. The word comes from the Gaelic *bean sí* meaning 'woman from the fairy mounds' or 'woman of the barrows'. Charlaine Harris' famous vampire books are filled with names from Celtic mythology and even refer to the fae themselves. Imagine the books at a tattoo artist's without

Celtic knots present, or a silversmith lacking the same. I had a good-natured argument with someone once who disputed the authenticity of anyone calling themselves 'Celtic'. I understood his point; we are not Celtic because the Celts are no more, if we take the word 'Celtic' to mean a part of a tribe of Celts. However, when I use the term 'Celtic' to describe a person or way of working, I take it as read that we understand already that the Celts are no more, and I am using this term to describe someone or something influenced in some way by some part of Celtic life.

As I write these chapters, I want to introduce you to a way of connecting with the world, even the universe, which harks back to the Iron Age and beyond; after all, our Celtic ancestors were themselves influenced by those who had come before. It's important to remember that the magic we perform today will never be the same as that of our ancestors; we are influenced by our ancestors, but we are not them. We live in a very different world, and we cannot pretend otherwise, but we can reach into the threads of time to try to understand the way magic affected those who came before, and we can search for those feelings and reactions in ourselves. To think that I may be feeling something as profound as one of my ancestors from over 2,000 years ago is heady indeed. We will look at simple steps towards being a Celtic witch from my own path, from very ethereal, meditative experience, to hands-on work using every-day items to aid spell-craft. We will discuss the Celtic reverence for the bard and satirist, and how you can learn to wield words as wisely, and how to cultivate silence as a weapon. We'll remember tales of magical transformation and wonder how we can transform ourselves. Do we want to change? Have we the will? And what is the consequence?

I opened this chapter with a triad that describes three things the wise should not do, but perhaps it is more positive to transform this (see, we are working magic already!) into three things a wise person should do: achieve the achievable, let things go which are harmful to us and be courageous. Many scholars have mulled over the meanings of Irish and Celtic triads. This particular one is Irish, to fit in with the flavour of my witchcraft style, and I find it easier to understand if you think of it in terms of what you can do rather than what you shouldn't.

Everything is achievable if you employ common sense and ambition. The first step to completing a task, is believing that you can do it. That's not enough, of course; you must work hard, plan where necessary and garner help when one person is not enough. But if you believe something is impossible, then it will become so. It is very easy to talk yourself out of something because it has become difficult. It is also easy to allow others to talk you out of something because, in their perception, you are attempting the impossible. Trust your instincts. Go with your gut. Above all, have faith that you would not feel your task was achievable without good reason. Belief in oneself is not airy-fairy or new age; it is confidence and it is necessary for all witchcraft. If you dither, you will not achieve your desired outcome. If you are foot-sure you will surely succeed.

I wouldn't agree that grieving over the irretrievable is pointless; grief is natural and part of the process of moving on. But we should not cling to that which is no longer with us. And we definitely shouldn't try to hold onto things that are bad for us. It's easy to think of this part of the triad in terms of death and loss. Try and take it to a smaller level. A task you failed to achieve; do you berate yourself constantly for it? Are you endlessly mad at yourself, going over and over what you could have done differently? It will be a different life before you can see that particular task again, if ever. You have two options; try again a different day, having learned from your errors. Or leave it and move on. Endlessly fretting will harm you, taking up valuable psychic and physical energy that could be spent doing other, more productive things. Every witch must learn at some point that you can't concentrate on something good when there is rubbish floating around the back of your head. Think of it as wiping the kitchen table before you prepare to cook. Your mind, your brain, is the source of your intent. Just like the food in the dirty kitchen, how can your intent be pure when you have filled your mind with despair and worry? Let it go.

The triad finally tells us not to fear the inevitable. Again, we are moved to consider death, and indeed most of those I know on a Celtic path consider death simply another step along a journey. A movement through the veil that separates the world we see on a day-to-day basis from the world of the fae. This may be a passing visit beyond the veil only to return in another incarnation. Or it may be a permanent move, depending on how much you have learned on this side of the veil. But death is not the only inevitability in this life. There are many things we can never be sure of or control; the weather, the actions of others and the behaviour of our chosen gods or spirits, just to name a few. So be confident in what you can change, let go of what you can't and do not be afraid to do nothing. Truly, if you rail against the inevitable or that which is outside of your control, you are wasting energy that could be better used for tasks that are achievable. Witchcraft is a collection of skills and the manipulation of magic, but it cannot achieve everything, nor should you expect it to. Be at peace with that which you cannot change, but be secure in the knowledge that you will damn well fight for what you need when the opportunity arises! The Celtic witch is a warrior and a sage, and as I continue this work I will try to show you how you can be both, and more, in the context of our modern world.

Chapter Two

Stepping Stones

Celtic Triad: Three candles that illumine every darkness: truth, nature, knowledge.

In magic we look to the elements, the directions and spirits among many, many other things, as a way to quantify and understand the universal energies we are harnessing. In Wicca and other rituals based on a similar foundation, the cardinal points are the focus for an individual or coven to consecrate or cast a circle: north, east, south and west, and their associated elements respectively: earth, air, fire and water. The practitioner can then go deeper to the aspects of the world associated with each element; birds of the air, or the heat of the summer sun for example.

Let's go deeper still to understand how the directions and elements represent different parts of human nature, or our own psyche. East is about new beginnings, birth, the start of something. The freshness of a morning breeze moves us towards thinking about the element of air. The carefree and uncontrollable nature of the wind; this translates in ourselves as mischief or playfulness, childishness or embracing our inner child and untempered emotions both light and dark. You'll note that I am careful to point out that each of these aspects has a flip side. There is no good and evil in Celtic witchcraft. Everything you do has consequences and you have to be prepared for that. It's up to you to make sure your choices affect your life and the lives of those around you in the way you intend. Hopefully this is a positive one! If you have darker designs, just remember consequences have a way of biting you in the bum when you least expect it.

At some point I'll provide the obligatory list of elemental correspondences and how you can use them, but it's important to note that I don't want you to feel bound by these. Celtic witchcraft is very much about using your instincts. Rite and ritual, tools and trinkets; these things are not necessary for you, but also they should not be shunned. Choose your own way of working, and expect it to change often, perhaps even daily at first. You are not only a witch; you are a scientist, experimenting with yourself and the world; responsibly, but with healthy curiosity and a sense of adventure.

By this point we have accepted that we are a part of a huge universe and a world that seems even huger because we are so close to it, even though in reality it is a tiny speck in the eye of creation. We use directions and symbolism to break this massive, incomprehensible world into smaller chunks that are easier to understand and, as we've discussed, we start to relate those pieces of the world to ourselves. How does this benefit us? Why do we need to do this? Ultimately, what's in it for you?

Well, what do you want? Why are you here? What answer eludes you? What desire is just out of reach? The Celts were seekers not only of knowledge, but also of wealth, power and beauty. I've found that there is no shame in admitting a desire for something worldly, just as there is certain glory in seeking something divine.

'This is the way of it then,' said Lugh. 'The three apples I asked of you are the three apples from the Garden in the East of the World, and no other apples will do but these, for they are the most beautiful and have the most virtue in them of the apples of the whole world. And it is what they are like, they are of the colour of burned gold, and they are the size of the head of a child one month old, and there is the taste of honey on them, and they do not leave the pain of wounds or the vexation of sickness on anyone that eats them, and they do

not lessen by being eaten forever.'
(*Gods and Fighting Men: The Story of the Tuatha de Danaan and of the Fianna of Ireland*; Gregory, Lady; John Murray, London, 1910)

Lugh, speaking here, has just lost his father. Instead of simply killing the culprits, the infamous Sons of Tuireann, he devises a plan whereby the murderers are sent on a mission that will either kill them through its sheer danger and difficulty or, if they somehow succeed, many great and powerful artefacts, such as the apples described above, will be bestowed upon Lugh. Lugh may seem somewhat cold to us; using his father's death as a vehicle to gain power. But look at it another way. He is distraught. His father, to whom he was very close, has been brutally taken from him. He can exact revenge, or he can use the situation positively. He masters his emotions and moves everyone down a path that ultimately can only end to his advantage.

This is basically how you have to think when you work with magic. You can't do magic angry. You can't do magic upset. Your intent has to be pure; not pure as in good, or even altruistic. But pure as in unsullied, not tainted by other thoughts and wishes that are roiling around inside your skull. You must master yourself before you can master magic. And that is why, as in all great endeavours, we start small.

Your journey is like crossing a river without a bridge. You must find the shallowest point, and use the water-worn rocks as stepping stone, to gradually move your way across. But before you even set foot upon a stone, let's sit on the bank awhile. Listen to the rush of the water. Appreciate its power. Look at the plants growing; there's a bulrush, oh and yellow flag... The water feeds and nourishes them. A dragonfly swoops down almost in tandem with a kingfisher; brilliant bolts of blue beneath the bright day. But look at how that piece of the opposite bank is crumbling away. The water is destroying it, minute by minute. This is what you have to understand about magic, and about witchcraft. It is power and the application of power. The former is a universal energy and the latter is a tool, a way of manipulating said energy. But you can never take it for granted and you will work hard before you ever feel that you have achieved a successful spell, or a change in the world. And you must never forget that power is only power; like the rush of the river, it has no alignment; no good, no evil. It is your intent that channels and directs the power, always.

So here we are, on the bank of this great body of water, thinking about what we need in order to be able to step confidently onto that first stone, with no fear of slipping. The triad tells us the candles that illuminate the darkness are truth, nature and knowledge. Truth is the first meal, and like breakfast, it's the most important one. Most importantly you have to be willing to face your own truth, your own desires, and the ability to be honest with yourself. What has brought you to this point? Why are you drawn to witchcraft? Are you trying to fix something in your life that you are unhappy with? This, I have often found, is not a great reason for learning any form of witchcraft. Magic is not a plaster or Band-Aid that can be put over the wounds in your life. Sure, it can help bolster your confidence and your ability to deal with difficulties, but it's not a cure-all. If all you want out of witchcraft is a way to cure unhappiness or misfortune, step away until you can come at it from a more balanced place. I have seen too many people delve deep into witchcraft to try to escape from the problems in their life, and it has never ended well. Witchcraft for revenge, for purely selfish reasons or as a kind of anti-depressant is ineffective at best and highly damaging at worst. You need a clear and uncluttered mind to do your best work in any endeavour. When you are working with magic, this is even more crucial, as the slightest crookedness in your intent can lead to unpredictable results.

Honesty with yourself is hard, but achievable. If you have any doubts about why you are doing what you are doing, address them head on. Don't be afraid of feeling doubt, or worry. These are normal, human emotions, and it would be more of a concern if you had no doubts or worry about learning witchcraft! There is another Irish triad that states:

Three things a person is: what he thinks he is, what others think he is and what he really is.

Try to address all three of these. What kind of a person do you think you are? Are you stubborn and headstrong? Or do you avoid confrontation? Are you kind and compassionate? Or out for number one? Then think of how others view you. This may sound harder, but think of a time a friend has described you to another. What personality traits were discussed? Were you flattered or riled? Did you feel like they had nailed you, to a tee, or were you shocked and surprised at the description? The purpose of this exercise is not to determine whether you are 'fit' to be a witch or walk a Celtic path, but simply to encourage you to explore the skill of self-analysis. It's really, really important that you can be as self-aware as possible, in order to be as honest as possible about your goals and ambitions. There are no right or wrong answers; please, please, please don't write yourself up as the kindest and most compassionate person in the world when actually you can't stand kids and you have a low tolerance for fools; every aspect of your personality is important and is a vital part of you. You will be the most complete person you can be when you accept every part of yourself and don't try to hide what you or others may see as 'dark' or 'negative'. Everyone (and I do mean everyone) has parts of themselves they are not proud of. However, those aspects may stand you in good stead at certain times in your life.

Think about a situation where you became angry, and that

anger helped you through the situation. Anger is often seen as a negative emotion, but the expression of anger is the outlet for depression, it can help overcome fear and it can drive us to actions that may seem out of character, but move us forward in some way.

I recently split with the father of my child, and it was my ultimately my anger that made me realise we were in the wrong place for each other. We had grown apart, and I didn't feel supported by him in any of my endeavours. Being fiercely independent, I tried not to let this bother me at first, but it's hard when the person who apparently loves you shows no interest in your achievements. I had spent so long being calm, collected and measured about every situation, that things had always settled down and seemed calm on the surface, though resentment and unease were constantly bubbling beneath. It wasn't until I lost my temper, said all the things I had been holding back from saying and truly threw down the gauntlet that it became clear that there was no fixing the problems that had grown between us. Without that outburst, that venting of steam, it's likely that we would still be struggling on together now, both unhappy and creating an unhappy home for our family. Anger was a cleansing force, although the experience was harsh, and extremely unpleasant, it was the emotional equivalent of ripping the plaster off the wound; painful but effective.

Hopefully you won't have to go through something as painful to appreciate that every aspect of you as a person will benefit you at some point in your life. But do try to make a note of the times when you are angry, sad, lonely, selfish, cruel, callous or apathetic; what's the impact this emotion is having on your life? How have your actions led to you behaving like this? And is there any way for you to turn this negative seeming behaviour into a positive force in your life? The answer will often be no, but the more you realise this, the easier it will become to stop this behaviour in its tracks; to stop yourself, take a breath, and make a different choice,

The second candle in the darkness is nature. Nature is a strange word; at its root it means 'how things are', the nature of things is their original state, how they began and even what they grow into. We've already discussed examining our own nature, but I feel that this section of the triad is referring to the more commonly accepted use of nature, the natural world. Wildlife. Plants. Animals. Weather. Landscapes. Everything that has barely been touched by mankind or technology and, indeed, remains somewhat in its original state. Why is it important to be in touch with nature? Almost every Pagan path holds reverence toward nature at some core point in its tenets, yet often the why and wherefore of this are not explored. As we move through this book, we will explore the different ways to connect with your local land, but for now, as we rest on the riverbank, all we need to understand is why it is important.

Well firstly, you are a part of the natural world. You are an animal; a mammal. If you take off your clothes and lie in the grass it is basically your shape and sentient thought that distinguishes you from the cows in the field. I'm not suggesting you do this! But you can if you want. Watch out for spiders; that's all I'm saying. My point is we are not better than the cow. We are not more important. We are one strand in a web of creation, which is a huge and complex web. I use the term web because it reminds us that everything is connected. Every action we make affects something in some way. This may seem obvious, but it surprises me how many people seem to bounce along through life completely oblivious to the impact they are having on the world. When you pause and consider your actions, you can truly appreciate that the smallest effort can have huge consequences.

I had a wasps' nest in the garden last year. It was a bit scary. My first instinct was: 'Argh, get rid of it!' But I took some time to sit in the garden and watch the wasps, and I discovered that they were not interested in me in the slightest. They were a slightly smaller breed than the usual 'chase you around a field' variety, and they were so focused on their own business that my family and I did not register on their radar one iota. They had a strict flight path, which they stuck to, over the pine trees and back. They had one entrance hole to the nest, which was rarely threatened. On the odd occasion I came too near with the grass strimmer, they would pour out and fly in formation around the site, but would not attack. It was pure defensive posturing. That year I barely had any aphids in the garden as the carnivorous wasps fed on them constantly. Although I was scared of the wasps, I managed to live harmoniously with them, because I didn't follow my knee jerk reaction, which was to destroy them out of fear. At the end of summer, I saw the queen crawling away from the then-defunct site, and I dug out the whole area to stop infestation the following year. Nothing was killed except aphids, which the wasps had a good year of feasting on, and I had a relatively pest-free garden.

I'm not suggesting you let your house and garden be overrun by animals of all kinds; of course not. Our lives and homes are important too, just as the lives of the wasps were important. But if there is a way to find balance, this is preferable to simply dominating the natural world because you can. A lack of action can sometimes be as powerful and profound as the greatest endeavour. There are small ways to connect to nature; feeding the birds, sitting in a forest, having a wild patch in your garden. But, more than anything, don't feel that simply because you are top of your local food chain, that you are better than any other living thing. You are vital, and important. But so is everything else.

Finally, the last candle that illuminates the darkness, or the final stretch before placing a foot upon the stepping stones across the river: knowledge. This is actually a very tricky one, as with any esoteric subject, there are no hard and fast facts; there is only that which most people agree on. You will read many books that will ring true with you now, but perhaps in later years you will have outgrown that way of thinking, and have your own knowledge that is truer and more relevant to you.

The knowledge I will impart comes equally from the mythology and history of the Celts and current, modern thinking on magic. I combine the two to create a way of working that is relevant in today's world, but gives honour to the ways of our Celtic forebears.

My final tip for this chapter is this: get a notebook. I'm not going to say 'journal' or 'book of shadows'; simply a notebook, so every time you learn something new that will help you along your path to become a witch, you can write it down, and revisit it from time to time. These notes are your stepping stones; each nugget of knowledge is a step across the river. Feel the rock beneath your feet, the fire of the blood pumping in your veins, the cool whisper of wind on your face and the force of flow around you as the river sings on. You will cross this fierce beast, and it will be your own hands and mind that allow you to do it. Be proud.

Chapter Three

Stopping the Clock, Losing the Calendar

Celtic Triad: Three sorrows that are better than joy: the heaviness of a herd feeding on mast, the heaviness of a ripe field, the heaviness of a wood under mast.

When does the Celtic year start? And more importantly, does it matter?

To the first question my answer is simply, I don't know. And really, nobody does. We are pretty certain, thanks to the wonderful find of the Coligny Calendar, that Samhain marked the end of summer and the beginning of winter, and many Pagans following a Celtic path have taken this to be their new year. Samhain is a liminal period between light and dark, when the potential for change and transformation is strong. So it makes sense that in an age where we are fixated on time and date, this would be the point at which we start the year anew.

Others suggest Imbolc, because of it being a celebration of birth and new beginnings. It is the world starting to come to life again. The first splashes of green on a dusty white canvas. The first bleats of lambs under the bright winter sun.

Of course, it's very possible that there was no Celtic New Year festival as such and that each season was marked and celebrated as another turn of the wheel, rather than a fixture within a year. It's even more likely that different Celtic tribes followed slightly different calendars to each other.

To the second question: does it matter? I don't think so. We are influenced by our ancestors, and in following a path of Celtic witchcraft we are trying to channel that inspiration into our day-to-day lives. However, this doesn't mean you are trying to be your ancestors. You are not trying to match, action for action, word for word, how your ancestors behaved, because if we do, what is the point of the human race growing and evolving? We reach back to touch our ancestors to understand ourselves better, and to keep alive the magic and traditions of the past. But we do so in our own lives, in a modern world. So don't get too hung up on dates and timings, and be prepared for lively debate with those who do!

So what is important in a Celtic witch's calendar? Not looking at one, for a start. To get in touch with the way your ancestors would have dealt with time and the seasons, it's worth trying to follow the days without resorting to dates on a piece of paper, or your smartphone. Don't lose touch completely – after all we still have to get to work or college on time and pick the kids up and so forth! But it's worth trying the following exercise to see if you can extend your senses into the world around you to feel the turn of the seasons rather than just note them by the date.

Moon Watching

We all know a cycle of the moon is about 28 days. You may have at some point celebrated on a full moon, or a new moon, or simply noticed the phase marked in your diary. But have you ever noticed the changes on a daily basis? Have you ever seen the moon from one day to the next and been astonished at the difference in size, colour and position?

For this exercise all you will need is a notepad (digital or otherwise) and the commitment to go outside for a few minutes every day or night. On any night when the sky is clear and the moon is visible, pop out and have a look.

What phase is the moon? Can you work out if she is waxing or waning? In the northern hemisphere, the moon waxes and wanes right to left, so if the changing 'bulge' is at the left, she is waxing, and if it is at the right, she is waning. If a crescent's horns are at the right, she is waning, and if the horns are at the left, she is waxing. This is the other way around in the southern hemisphere.

Try to figure out where you are in the moon's cycle simply by looking at the moon. Write down as much as you can; the shape, the position, the colour; is there a halo? What is the weather like? Are there any stars visible? Can you recognise any constellations? Is it just after sunset, late at night or early in the morning? What time of year is it? Close your eyes and let the moonlight wash over you. What thoughts enter your head? How does it make you feel? Finally, make a note of your general mood through the day.

The next day, cloud cover permitting, do the same again. Try to go out around the same time, but don't clock watch; if you went out last night just after sunset, do the same again. If it was just before supper time, this is good enough too. You are trying to achieve a natural rhythm, rather than a strict routine.

Note any changes. Has the position of the moon changed? How about the colour and size? You may be able to confirm if she is waxing or waning at this point, if you weren't sure the previous night. You may notice that the moon isn't visible at all, and if so, keep an eye out the next day for her being visible in the daytime sky.

If you keep repeating this exercise on a daily basis, one day you will go out and realise that the moon is the same phase as when you began the exercise. You will feel surprised that 28 to 29 days has gone by, because you haven't been thinking, 'Gosh, I have to do this for a month!' It has just been a few minutes each day, fitted in between your normal routine.

Again, note the details of the moon and the moonlit night, and most importantly, how you have been feeling that day and how you feel right now, under the moon's gaze. Now flick back through your notes and compare this day with that first day. Are there any similarities? Was your mood very similar that day, or completely different? How has the weather changed? Has the season turned warmer or colder in that time? How has one turn of the moon affected your world? Can you feel that your local environment has changed in that time? Perhaps leaves have started to fall, or at the other end of the year perhaps you can see green buds where there were none before. Perhaps there is still a glow on the horizon from the lateness of the sunset, or a deeper black to the night sky as the evening closes in earlier.

Have you noticed any changes in yourself? Perhaps you are sleepier, or more relaxed, or tense, or excited. You have success-fully used one entire 'moon', a proper month, to note changes not just in the world around you, but in yourself. You have a person-alised almanac that can be referred back to again and again to help you extrapolate what may be happening at the same phase of the moon in the future, and at this time of year in the years to come.

I recommend keeping this exercise up for a few months as it's really useful to see how your mood changes with the phases of the moon. You may find there is no correlation at all, but the chances are you will look back at your notes and see similar feelings and states of mind jotted at around the same phases of the moon. There are many books and sites that state 'you will be reflective around the new moon' or 'the full moon will bring stress', but the point is that everyone is affected by the moon differently. Noting how the moon affects you and your local surroundings will make you a more powerful witch, as you know when you are at your strongest and when you should rest or meditate. Here are some of my most common findings about myself throughout the differing phases of the moon.

Dark Moon (Not Visible)

A time for reflection and planning. I often meditate around this time and note the imagery that arises. I find answers flow from the darkness, and in the absence of light I can see further into myself than normal, if I can unwind enough and give myself the time to do so. I feel relaxed, sometimes even lazy. I can get mad at myself for letting tasks slip by.

New Moon (Tiny Sliver, Waxing)

I plant seeds at the new moon, physical and metaphysical! In gardening season I really feel the urge to get out and plant and plan and make the garden ready for the season to come. In the darker months I write lists and feel very practical, although I can become so bogged down in the planning that I take too long to actually get on with the 'doing'.

Waxing Crescent

Sometimes I will start new projects around this phase, often of a creative nature. My band was started on a waxing crescent and has been a great source of joy for both of us involved. Sometimes I will take on too many tasks, and feel under pressure. I can become very focused on one particular task to the detriment of others, although I will always realise this and rush to rectify my mistakes if any have been made.

Half-Moon, Waxing

My emotions are up and down, either very low or very up. This seems to be a time of extremes for me. I can get myself het up about not finishing projects or not getting started with tasks that have deadlines coming up soon. For me, the best thing to do is to make some time to meditate and calm down. It's a time where I have to check my priorities carefully, and make sure I say 'no' if I really don't have time to do things.

Waxing Gibbous (Bulging to the Left in the Northern Hemisphere)

I feel renewed and energised. This has always been my favourite phase of the moon, ever since I was a child. All through my life I have looked up and seen the fat, but not yet full, moon as a friend and happy companion. I feel joy, kindness and a connection to the world that may not have seemed possible a few days before. This is my most productive phase, but also a phase where I won't get angry at myself for resting or recuperating if needed.

Full (May Seem Full for 2 or 3 Days)

I feel very aware of my surroundings at the full moon, particularly if the moon is visible; the sight of the full moon excites me, which of course sharpens the senses. I will often simply stand in my garden gazing at the moon, feeling the wind on my face, noting the temperature and the night sounds and becoming a part of the night itself. I'm also aware that others struggle at the full moon, so I feel a great deal of compassion around this time, and will always pick the phone up straight away in case it's someone in need of a friendly shoulder.

Waning Gibbous (Bulging to the Right)

Strange things seem to happen to me at this phase of the moon. I may bump into someone I have not seen for a while, or lose something that turns up again inexplicably. A time of mystery and mischief.

Half-Moon, Waning

A sense of contentment fills me, troubles are easily dealt with and happy times have an even brighter tinge than normal. I feel confident and lustrous.

Waning Crescent

I tend to feel a sense of positive anticipation, like something good or interesting is about to happen. If well, I am physically active and want to get loads done. If I have a cold around this phase of the moon it tends to hit me hard and leaves my body feeling drained and tired, though my mind is active and wants to play!

Old Moon (Tiny Sliver, Waning)

This tends to be my time for checking over things, making sure things have been done properly; not second guessing myself, simply being thorough and meticulous. I can also be like this with others, which can make me a bit grouchy and pernickety. I'm not always the best company at this time!

So there you have it, this is me at different phases of the moon. What will your journal look like? You'll probably find it's completely different. After all, noting the changing of the moon is simply a way to record the passing of time. It doesn't follow that a waxing crescent will show the same mood in you as I, because your own individual, internal cycle is bound to be completely different to mine.

As a witch, you can use this information about yourself to plan your magical exploits. For example, I normally won't try to do healing work around a waxing half-moon, because my emotions are very up and down and my focus will not be where it should be. I would rather do this type of work around the waning half-moon, when I feel confident and relaxed, and can therefore focus all my energy and intent on the person who needs it, rather than being distracted by my own personal struggles.

At the old moon, the tiny sliver before it becomes briefly invisible, I can be found tidying altars and straightening my work area out. I take my 'pickiness' and turn it into a positive; spending hours making sure an incense blend is perfect for a particular rite, for example. Waxing a piece of wood to a shine for a staff or wand, or picking just the right amount of herbs from the garden for an offering.

Whatever magic you want to work, whether that means changes in yourself, in others or in the world around you, knowing yourself is the best way to get the most out of yourself. It sounds obvious, but so many magical practitioners believe they can go through the motions and achieve the same results every time, without considering their own mood, wellbeing and their local surroundings.

Following the above exercise and keeping a moon journal has the following benefits:

a) You will always know what the phase of the moon is. It will become second nature.
b) You will gain a huge insight into your own emotional and physical cycles.
c) You can use this knowledge to perform the best and most effective witchcraft.
d) You will see and understand the change of the seasons and only use a calendar for appointments!

As you keep your journal, note the first time you see a leaf turn red, or fall from a tree. Mark the first apple blossom, or the first storm of cherry petals that blow across your windows. Note the lengthening of the day, and the chill departing on a night. Try to feel the change in the season, rather than just knowing it is happening.

A Journal of the Seasons

As I write this chapter, it is early autumn and the maple trees at my son's school are putting on a stunning show. The reds and purples and oranges don't seem possible; they are so bright and such a surprise after the glossy green of the hot and damp summer. I can smell the turn in the air; the smell of moist earth (actinomycete spores rising from the soil cause this smell, so don't think you're imagining it!), the smell of ozone as the weather systems change and the smell of the leaves starting to decay upon the ground. This is a time for foraging, making remedies to last the winter, and preparing for festivities and fun at the Autumn Equinox and Samhain.

When autumn turns to winter I know there will be a cold, crisp smell in the air that promises snow (and often doesn't deliver) as well as a whiteness to the sky instead of the grey, shuffling clouds of the moment. Darkness will overtake light and will have its peak at Yule, the Winter Solstice, halfway between the Celtic festivals of Samhain and Imbolc. The magic of personal growth is strong at this time, and you may plant the seeds that you wish to blossom in the coming spring; a new goal, an ambition, or simply to become kinder, more compassionate, or have more self-confidence. Now is the time to work on those aspects of yourself.

As Imbolc approaches I will be focused on staying warm and toasty, and getting together with friends and family, and my magical colleagues, to make sure everyone is OK and not struggling through the darker season. This is the time to be a community witch; to look out for the weak and vulnerable, or the strong and steady who are simply having a bad time! This is a time for the practical magic of conversation, a helping hand and hot food where needed. I will be supporting my local homeless community, to try to make sure as many mouths are fed as possible.

As the season turns green again, the smell of damp earth returns, along with the warm musk of animal dung as the sheep and cows return to pasture. In cities, trees lining the streets will start to be tinged with green, and the birds will start singing earlier. Baby starlings will be cheeping, and male pigeons will be puffing out their chests hopefully. Early spring is a time of massive potential, and you can do practically anything at this time. Write music, sing, dance, walk in the woods, talk to animals, meditate, journey, heal, craft, cook; whatever your skill is, you will find a space for it around the birthing of a green and renewed world.

Then pale green becomes perfectly emerald under a sapphire sky as summer glints into view. The heat and excitement bubble inside me, and even on rainy days in summer I can feel my energy vibrating. The garden grows wild and stresses me out, and hot days can leave me feeling a bit wobbly and drained, but in general summer is a time for being outside as much as possible, staying up late to see the moon and stars, going camping, outside ritual, visiting standing stones, travelling as much as possible and writing and creating as often as I can.

Only you can know what kind of a witch you are or will be, and I hope this chapter will helps you with that self-discovery. In the next chapter we will look at the colours of Celtic magic, and how these appear in our day-to-day lives, and how you can use them in your witchcraft. But, for now, think on the day; think on the season; think on the moon. Forget the clock and lose the calendar, just for a little while.

Chapter Four

Colour me Red (and Black and White...)

We've examined how to feel the turn of the world around us. Now it's time to look at some of the detail. Let's get a bit closer to the magic surrounding us every day.

Colour is a fundamental part of our modern world, used in signs, warnings, adverts, clothes and more to send a multitude of messages. Yet this is not a new device. For thousands of years colour has been used to symbolise emotion, magic and hidden meanings. The three colours often associated with Celtic magic and mythology are red, white and black, and in this chapter we will examine why, and how to utilise this knowledge.

Red

The colour red appears throughout Celtic mythology and is normally associated with magic in some way. This may be the prophecy of war and bloodshed. Rowan, the tree with the startling red berries, is strongly associated with powerful magic. The Morrígan herself is normally portrayed as having red hair, especially in her guise as a sorceress or poet. Red is the magic of spells, curses, geas and predictions. Red is proactive magic; visible magic; magic that wants to be seen, admired or feared.

Think about red in our daily lives. Red means stop; warning; danger; love; passion; blood; fire; forbidden; command; hang up; hot; hazard and generally 'pay attention right now'. It is the colour of compulsion. We are almost programmed to pay attention when we see red. The term itself, 'seeing red', denotes a state of rage that implies we are no longer fully in control of ourselves. In nature, flowers are red to attract pollinators, and insects are often red (or red and black) to warn of venom, or to con predators into thinking the potential prey is dangerous.

Birds may flash red feathers to attract a mate and among our own 'plumage', red is considered a sexy colour; racy, dangerous and daring.

Fire

Red is used as the colour of the direction of south, and the element of fire. Often a red candle is placed at the southern part of an altar, or the southernmost part of a room where magical work is practised. It may, however, not be practical for you to use fire or indeed to have candles in places where small hands or paws can reach them. So, instead, you may want to use a red ribbon, symbolising the way passion binds us. A red pen can symbolise the fire of creativity. A simple blob of red paint on a stone or shell may bring a Spartan and natural beauty to your sacred space. You can use red flowers from the season; poppies in spring, roses in summer, perhaps chrysanthemums or rudbeckia in autumn and perhaps amaryllis or similar in winter.

Other natural additions to a sacred space can be hawthorn berries, rowan berries or holly berries depending again on the season. The juice from elder berries can be used to stain things red, and can even be used as a sort of ink.

Passion

Our passions are not just the obvious trio of love, desire and lust. We all have passions that stretch into other aspects of our lives; our ambitions, our motivation and our goals. Using red in magic helps us reach out from a place of wanting to a place of having or being. Red is also the connection between the human, physical state and the ethereal, magical state. When you are performing magic, you can imagine red blood flowing through an umbilical cord that attaches you to the universe, combining your own energy with that which resides within everything.

If you feel like you have taken on too many tasks, and can't find a way to prioritise, this exercise is useful. Find a quiet and calming space. Make it feel comfortable; light incense, play music or open a window. Whatever makes you feel more *you* is very important here. Draw a red spiral on a white piece of paper. Start at the edge of the paper and working inwards from the top left corner, draw the curve clockwise and spiral gently in to the centre. There is no rush. Let the thoughts of the tasks you have piled upon yourself wash through your mind, without focusing on one in particular. While these thoughts flow, keep your eyes following the spiralling line you are drawing. When your spiral reaches a central point, focus on the whole image, then close your eyes and breathe deeply. You should find that you are able to prioritise much more easily, and also that the feelings of stress and pressure have alleviated. You are refilled with a passion to achieve your goals, instead of the fear that you won't.

Blood

The colour red sneaks into magical and healing practice all over the world. Red is the colour of blood and therefore is intrinsically linked to life, and of course all that goes with that: passions, emotions, health, sickness and even death.

This is a technique I learned through my study of the ancient Mexican practice of Curanderismo. When you are feeling particularly stressed out, carry a piece of red ribbon in your pocket. Whenever a problem crops up, tie a knot in the ribbon, concentrating on the issue that gripes at you. At the end of the day, take the ribbon out of your pocket. Look at all the knots. These are your problems. There may be few; there may be many. Go out into the garden, or if you don't have a garden, use a pot on your windowsill. Bury the ribbon and imagine letting go of all your problems. You are returning the physical representation of your troubles to the earth. Letting go physically helps you to let go mentally.

Black

Black is not as evocative as red. We use black to delineate and to emphasise, rather than as the primary colour. It is the colour of boundaries and edges; the threshold between spaces. Black highlights the moment of change or transformation. We now know black is the absence of light and therefore the absence of colour. It's doubtful our Celtic ancestors understood this, but they had the insight to know that the black shadows that swept across fields both green and bloody were not just crows and rooks, but messengers between the worlds. If we think of black as an absence, then it is a void; a portal in the world. Every patch of pure black is the opportunity to send energy into the ether and have it transformed in some way.

Black is generally used in mediaeval and later texts concerning Celtic mythology to denote evil, for example in Keating's *History of Ireland* we are told of the 'Black Fleet' that comes to Cruachain, at the time Seadna, king of Ireland, is killed by his own son. One of the Celtic triads speaks of three 'black' husbandries: thatching with stolen things, putting up a fence with a proclamation of trespass, kiln drying with scorching. The term black in both these cases is used to imply bad fortune and ill winds. However, if we look at the source of this assumption, we must remember these manuscripts use the language of their time. The Celts may have seen the omens as bad, but it is later scholars who have chosen the term 'black' to emphasise the evil inherent. It is therefore more useful to look at the imagery in Celtic mythology to understand the nature of black: the black of the crow or raven; evaporating water described as black vapour (black here meaning invisible); creatures described as black when they usually would not be to highlight their unique nature.

An old wart treatment from County Tyrone, documented in the *Rosa Anglica* was:

If you meet a black snail accidently, rub it on the wart and stick the snail on the first thorn you meet.

And

If you lick a black snail when suffering from toothache you will be certainly cured.

The colour black clearly indicates some sort of healing property here. Rivers about to burst are often described as 'black'. As well as mirroring a stormy image, the term black here also implies fullness, fertility and a moment of crisis or completion.

Feidelm, the prophetess in *Táin Bó Cúailnge*, is described as having black eyebrows, black eyelashes and two black horses, associating black with the power of words and prophecy. Lugh is described as carrying a black shield when Cú Chulainn meets him for the first time, associating the colour with protection and defence. This association is deepened when Lugh dons a black charioteer's mantle in order to help Cú Chulainn fight.

As part of the triad of colours, often used by Pagans on many different paths, black is the obvious counterpart to white and therefore a symbol of balance, unity and the cyclical nature of all things.

A Black Circle

Sprinkle ground charcoal to mark a protective circle, as well as any other protective elements you may use. The black is a definitive border; a visible edge that helps focus all participants. It serves to protect and connect to the other-worldly. If on a firm surface outdoors, you could even draw the circle in charcoal. Just don't get in trouble for defacing someone's property!

A Black Stone

If you find a black stone while out and about, pocket it. Make a note of where you found it. Was it at the beach, glossy and wet?

Was it hiding at the foot of a tree? Or simply loose on a city path? Place the stone at an appropriate place on your altar or in your sacred space. The obvious choice is somewhere north facing, to strengthen the association with earth. But you may find the stone resonates more with the ocean, and therefore water, or perhaps the fire of creativity from within a bustling town. Follow your gut. If you decide to do a spell for someone, you can give them this stone to keep on their person or in a place significant to them. Then when you are working on your intent, you can focus on the stone that is now familiar to you as a way of connecting with that person, who will be doing the same. The stone becomes a way of linking the person's desire with your own intent, and can sometimes amplify the result.

Example

I gave my friend a black stone from my altar, and the following instructions: 'Every night, place the stone somewhere in the eastern corner of your room (this stone had strong associations of air for me) and light a candle. Just focus on the stone, and think about what it is you want. Don't worry if other thoughts come and go, just make sure this is the main hub your thoughts revolve around.'

Each night, at the same time, I would enter my sacred space and focus on what she had asked me to do. In this instance, this was to help resolve a conflict that was brewing. I focused on the image of the stone, and my own candle light. I imagined her sitting there, doing the same. I thought about her gaining clarity of thought, wisdom, and the courage to fight with wit and words should it be necessary. I visualised the happy ending she desired, but also reminded her that she would be okay if things did not turn out the way she wanted. I imagined the stone passing this intent on to her, as she sat and contemplated her problems.

The situation was resolved and mostly happily; she didn't shy away from the difficult situation and when the stone returned to me I moved it to the south of my space to represent the fires of determination.

A Black Feather

When you find a black feather, pick it up and keep it. These are normally corvid feathers, the feathers of the Morrígan's messengers: crows, rooks, ravens, jackdaws, magpies and jays among others. Use them to represent air on your altar or in a sacred space. They also represent the boundaries between things, messages from the other-world or land of the dead, and cleansing. Corvids are scavengers, but this means they eat many things we see as waste, so they are actually nature's cleaners. The world would be a much smellier place without them!

Use a bunch of black feathers to sweep your hearth at Samhain, to sweep away the summer and welcome your ancestors. Similarly, you can use them to dust a sacred space at any time, to imbue the place with the intent to use it for magic or other-worldly reasons.

In an evocation to the Morrígan, black feathers, particularly crow feathers, may be burnt in an open fire with a chimney or on an outside fire as an offering and welcoming. The smoke must be able to escape as you are sending a signal of invitation and if that is trapped within your home it is ineffective. And burning feathers don't particularly smell nice! Similarly, in any ritual setting, black feathers may be used to represent the Morrígan or any of her sisters/counterparts: Badb, Macha or Nemain.

A Black Cloth

A black ribbon on your door handle is an excellent way to let your loved ones know you are busy, plus it helps protect your space.

Wearing a black belt or cord can give you confidence if you are feeling anxious, particularly about transitions. Maybe you are starting a new job, or moving house. Or maybe you are changing a course of study, or even something emotionally dramatic like leaving a lover. Think about how black is a boundary, yet also invisible. You wear the black to remind you that although things are changing around you, you are the same person and you only change on your own terms. The black also represents the unknown things you are going into – the unseen. Wearing the black shows the courage to face the unknown head on, and this will make you feel that courage deep within you.

A Black Space

Find an outdoor space where you are comfortable and feel safe. This is ideal at a campsite where you are surrounded by friends. I don't recommend this exercise if you feel the place you are going to presents danger of any kind. Find a comfortable place to sit. Take a blanket or a cushion; you will be sat for a while so bring whatever you need to be comfy for this period. If you have the time and patience, I recommend starting at dusk, but if not, do this just after full sunset.

Use a torch to find a good place to sit, where you are safe and calm. Sit, relax, and switch your torch off. Simply exist in the dark. Concentrate only on your breathing, and then as you relax fully, extend your senses to the world around you. Take a deep breath through your nose and note each smell. The aroma of earth, damp and organic. Perhaps there is a note of wood smoke from a campfire. The tang of pine sap melting from ancient trunks. The oddly warm musk of cow dung from the surrounding fields.

What can you hear? Here and there are rustles in the hedgerows. Mice perhaps, or voles. A twig cracks, evidence of a larger animal, perhaps a rabbit or a hare. Are there any birds still calling? Or perhaps you can hear the first owls of the night calling to each other, ethereal and hidden among the trees; the same trees that you can hear whispering with voice of leaf and creak of branch; limbs reaching for the moon, stark and black against the black-blue sky.

Look into the blackness of the tree's silhouette. See if you can see any definition at all. Has the night robbed the great plant of all its detail? Or perhaps you can see the roughness of bark or parting of trunk as your eyes get used to the dark. Note the contrast between the tree and the sky; the edges of the tree's outline. Perhaps the moon is framed between its branches. Think of the black and darkened tree as a bridge between earth and sky; forever grounded but eternally reaching. Imagine yourself this way: deep and honest in your intent and principles, but always looking to improve, to connect with the universe, and to become better than you are: forever growing and changing.

White

White is the Celtic colour of mystery and magic. Unlike black, it is not usually found in a liminal state, but signifies that magic is now taking place; that we have moved beyond transition and become transformed. It is not bound in the physical world like the colour red; it stands apart from emotion and desire and is a power all of its own. Although used by humans on ritual clothing and tools for many millennia, white does not need interaction with human hands in order to signify magic.

We see white creatures as unusual or lucky. White horses (normally called 'greys') are considered special, and legendary figures such as Rhiannon, from Welsh Celtic mythology, appear in our world riding such a creature. Rhiannon, often associated with Gaulish horse goddess Epona, seems to ride in on the beautiful, pure white creature to appear next to a burial mound, strongly suggesting their association with the world of the fae. Hunting a white creature often leads the hunter to encounter magic; sometimes good, sometimes not.

The hounds of the underworld are supposedly white with red ears. One may immediately say, 'Oh well, white must be associated with death then!', but it is the red of the ears that signifies the human and visceral experience of dying. The white of the main body of the dog signifies that is a purely magical creature, merely connected to humanity by its abode in the realms of those who have died.

A white candle is used as a central point for ritual or on an altar because white is the culmination of the other colours. White is all colour, and all light, so magically white indicates a central point of power. It is potential, and marks the point at which we are aware we are working with forces beyond the mundane.

White is also the colour of salt, used as a traditional tool of protection for many centuries.

A white feather falling from the sky onto the path in front of you is a message from one who has passed on. Normally this will occur shortly after the person or animal's death, as a way of letting you know they have arrived safely where they need to be. Often these feathers will be the soft downy feather of a goose or swan fledgling, indicating the start of a new journey. You can take this feather home and keep it safe, perhaps displayed in the eastern part of your home or sacred space. Or you can simply close your eyes, hold the feather while you remember the person concerned, then breath out and with that sigh, let the feather back into the wind to continue its journey.

As a writer, a blank, white sheet of paper can be incredibly magical indeed. The paper in front of me is the medium of magic, and the lines I pen onto it are the witchcraft; the manipulation of that magic. Sometimes I will write in a combination of black and red, with red used for names of deities, spirits or places of significance. The black words are my own thoughts; my own boundary between what is in my mind and what is real. The red words are names that do not come directly from me, but still hold weight and power and so influence my behaviour, thought and emotion. Red is the combination of the other-worldly and my own energy. White is neither my work, nor the work of any spirit; it is the magic inherent in the universe. White is the potential for magic, the doorway to magic, and magic itself.

Think of how these colours appear in your day-to-day life. Something as simple as a zebra crossing, for example. The black stripe of Tarmac highlighting your transition from one place to another, and the liminal state you are in while still on the dangerous road. The white is the bright colour that glares at the drivers, protects you and marks the area as special. Of course, zebra crossings were almost definitely not designed with Celtic magic in mind! But, by looking at everyday things in this way, you can pull these ideas into your own witchcraft to make it more effective and useful.

To complete our thoughts on Celtic colour magic, take three cords or long ribbons, one each of red, black and white. Tie them securely at the top, and plait them. Do this slowly, all the while thinking of what each colour means to you; the protection, the liminality, the passion. Make it personal to you. Hang this triple cord above the entrance to your sacred space. It will remind you of the triple nature of things; that every situation has more than one perspective and every choice has more than one consequence. It will remind you of the many-faceted nature of magic, and how colours can represent this and aid you by focusing your intent. But mostly it will remind you that you can create effective magic with your own hands. Never forget that you hold power within you, and the colours, cords and creativity are all channels for that power. It's up to you to find the channel that works best for you.

Chapter Five

An Elemental Thing...

Magic, and therefore witchcraft, is intrinsically intertwined with the elements. In most western traditions, we look to the four 'classical' elements of earth, air, fire and water. These are often associated with the respective cardinal points of the compass: north, east, south and west. In Wicca and associated paths, there is also the central point, the culminating element, spirit, that represents the centre of existence and the energy within the universe.

This is not constant throughout all cultures, though. In Japanese Buddhism, for example, the element of 'spirit' is known as 'void' and can also represent the sky or heaven. In the Chinese philosophy Wu Xing, the five critical agents that cause all things to interact are wood, fire, earth, metal and water. These agents, or phases, are often associated with the four seasons and the cycle of all things. Within alchemy, the three basic materials are salt, sulphur and mercury; perhaps not what most of us would automatically think of as the foundation of all existence!

The common denominator with all these short lists of key ingredients is that they are all familiar to the philosophers in question. We breathe air, we use fire, we drink water and we live in and on the earth. Or, from a different perspective, we live under the sky, we are afraid of fire, we bathe in water, and we are made of earth.

So what are the Celtic elements? The Celts lived in the same world we did; living from the earth, relishing the sun and either railing against or celebrating the weather, depending on the season. The Celts moved across continents, absorbing aspects of the cultures they encountered and sharing aspects of themselves in the same way. It is therefore difficult to say with certainty which elements or aspects of the universe would have influenced the Celts most, because each Celtic tribe was different and held its own beliefs and customs. There is no primary Celtic religion or philosophy that overrides all others.

However, we can extrapolate some information from the stories and legends retold by scholars of the Celts. As always, when reading these stories for yourself, look to the source; a Christian monk writing in the Middle Ages will skew the story to a pro-Christian viewpoint, for example. Take everything with a pinch of salt and form your own opinions.

Pools of Wisdom

Celtic myth and legend is certainly not short of a few stories about rivers, fords, wells, springs and lakes. Water is one element that we can state, with reasonable confidence, was important to the Celts not only for staying alive, but also as part of their spirituality. Water is intrinsically linked to wisdom, occult knowledge and hidden mysteries. Tales range from the legend of Boann, who challenges the power of the Well of Segais and is killed in the creation of a new river, to the archetypal image of the 'washer at the ford' and the association with prophecy and the afterlife. It is impossible to examine Celtic religion without including the significance of water.

Today, in the western world, we take the availability of clean water for granted, but many of us, particularly city dwellers, may only ever interact with water from a tap or a bottle. It's well worth your time to visit your nearest water source and get a feel for the environment there. Listen to the buzz of insects. Watch the water birds serenely gliding, or not so serenely squabbling! Watch out for the shadows of fish gliding beneath the surface tension, causing mysterious ripples around tall, whippy reeds and great, flat lilies. Catch the tail whip of a water vole, or the unearthly blue arrow flash of a kingfisher. Breathe through your nose and take note of the smell. A stagnant pool may smell dank and unpleasant, whereas a free-flowing river will smell fresh and almost earthy. You may even smell the scents of some of the flowers growing on the banks.

What amazes me is the absolute abundance of life around these places. Water is a life-giver, both as a source of hydration and as a breeding ground for bacteria. Even the search for extra-terrestrial life is generally the search for possible water-bearing planets, because of the fundamental understanding that life (as we know it) cannot exist without water.

But water is also a destroyer. You can drown in water – and not even that much of it. According to Keating, the druids of the Tuatha Dé Danann raised a mighty storm in order to drown the sons of the invading Míl Espáine. Drowning is also mentioned as capital punishment in *The Death-Tales of the Ulster Heroes* (tr. Kuno Meyer, 1906) although in this particular tale the criminal is a poet who chooses to be drowned when caught 'co-habiting' with Conchobar mac Nessa's wife.

Water also destroys simply by existing. A river erodes its banks; a waterfall carves into a cliff face; even persistent rain over centuries wears at rock and earth and changes it irrevocably. You only have to visit a place like Brimham Rocks in North Yorkshire to see the devastating yet beautiful impact water has had over aeons, forming incredible structures out of the local geology.

From the last paragraph we can surmise that water is also patient, industrious, persistent; even stubborn. These are all characteristics you can associate with water in your own working.

Take a bath. Make it perfect; just the right temperature and fill level to induce complete relaxation. While you lay, partially submerged, think about the water that surrounds you. Where did it come from? Once it was in the sky. Before that it was under the ground, and it will return to the ground again, and one day will be part of the sky again. Reflect upon the cyclical nature of things. Think about your own journey through life; how you constantly change, yet are the same person. Like the water, you move from situation to situation, but you are the same soul; the same heart. Think about the fluid nature of the water you float in. It adapts to its environment; it is shaped by its container yet can change at a moment's notice. Are you as adaptable? How does this make you feel? A slight breath on the water makes it ripple, just like you are stirred by external events. The surface of the bath water is like your emotions; it can be still or chaotic depending on the stimuli.

Water is a fascinating substance; it exists as a solid, a liquid and a gas and we regularly use all three forms. Water heals, water kills, water dreams and water thrills. The Celts simply accepted the magical nature of water, and science has since proven how utterly remarkable it is. Find your own special connection to water, and see where the flow of the river takes you.

Winds of Wyrd

Yeats insisted in 1933 that the sídhe, or Celtic spirits, had 'much to do with the wind' because the word sídhe means wind. Sorry William, it doesn't. However, sídhe gaoithe is the Gaelic term for a whirlwind, or dust devil, sometimes associated with the 'fair folk' as it was believed they could travel on the swirling air.

I have seen a small dust devil pick up and distribute pink cherry blossom into the most glorious and impossible looking display, so can completely understand how one could believe the phenomena is controlled by a supernatural force. Or perhaps the sídhe don't control the wind at all, but simply jump on and enjoy, wherever the ride may take them.

It is this carefree and child-like attitude that I tend to associate most strongly with air. The ability to take risks and to enjoy life. To revel in mischief, but with compassion and genuine care for those around you. To dare to sing and dance as the mood takes you. To peek and peer and explore the world around you with an entirely open mind.

Exploration often leads to understanding, and this is the other aspect of air I identify strongly with; clarity and intellectual stimulation. A stiff breeze can blow the cobwebs away and, if you imagine the musty corridors of your mind being dusted down by a refreshing summer breeze, you get a sense of how this element can help you order your thoughts and focus your intent.

Intent is so important in witchcraft. Going through the motions is not enough; you must believe firmly in what you are doing and the reason you are doing it. Anyone can recite a spell, or light incense, or tie knots. But a true witch examines what they want, how they are going to get it and most of all, why they are using witchcraft to get it. Air is the element of reason, which allows you to follow this process logically. It prevents you from hiding things from yourself, forcing you to examine your own self-doubt and either dismiss it, or trust it, depending on the situation.

Air can be the strongest wind or the smallest breath. Air constantly surrounds us and obviously we cannot live without it, but like the other elements it has its destructive nature too. As well as a breeze blowing away cobwebs, air can be a mighty hurricane or a tornado. Air can be youthful and jovial, but also commands respect. Find this capacity in yourself; to be both the howling storm and the calm breeze; the zephyr in the grass. Accept that you will be buffeted from time to time and don't be afraid to buffet back!

Green and Wild

Paganism in general leans towards a reverence for nature, which I tend to find stems from a genuine appreciation of the world around us rather than any particular religious pull. It's an obvious conclusion that if we look after Planet Earth, then as a species we have a better chance of surviving longer and enjoying a better quality of life. This means respecting not only the other creatures in this world, but the plants, the waterways, the air and every eco system.

Animists believe that everything has a spirit; every rock, every tree and even the weather. Juliette Wood, in her introduction to the 2000 edition of *Mythology of the British Islands* (Charles Squire, 1905) suggests that the Celts also held these beliefs. Whether this is true or not, the legends and stories surrounding place names, particularly in Ireland, lend credence to the theory that the Celts held the land in general and specifically their own locality in reverence.

Being familiar with your environment is absolutely essential for a witch. Understanding the energy of the soil beneath your feet, or perhaps beneath the concrete, will give you a foundation to build storey upon storey of magical success. Become familiar with how the seasons affect where you live. I'm fairly suburban, so I'm lucky enough to have a fair amount of green around me: my own garden (tiny though it is), brambles, fields and trees are only a few steps away. For me then, the turn of the seasons is a change of palette as green turns to gold turns to brown and back again.

Speak to your neighbours; learn anecdotes about the area you call home. You might find someone who knows when your house/flat/apartment was built. They might be able to tell you what was there before. You may even find old photos online of what the area looked like before being built upon. Imagine yourself on the same spot, but at different points throughout the ages. The people and technologies change, but the earth remains more or less the same. The earth is consistency, dependability, stubbornness; steadfastness.

I attended a 'coming of age' ceremony where the young man was given a gift of earth. This was literally a small, beautiful glass bottle, filled with earth from the family's garden. The mother told him he would always know where home was and always be able to find his way back. I love this idea, of taking a little piece of home with you, and also the metaphor that you already carry your home with you – in your heart and in the things you love.

Take a pot of local soil if possible, potting compost if not! Place a seed (any seed really, you're going to grow this indoors so it doesn't really matter about the type) about a centimetre deep (or follow packet instructions) and tamp the soil down. Imagine your intent is the seed. Just like the seed only exists within the earth, your intent only exists within you. Yet just like the seed will expand beyond the earth, the right additions will allow your intent to become reality. Water the seed lightly, and imagine what will nourish your desire. Keep those thoughts of how to bring your intent to fruition firmly in mind. Pop a food bag (or any small plastic bag) over the pot and place on a bright window sill. Check daily. Moisture will collect on the inside of the bag and run back down in the pot so there should be little need for further watering, but if the soil starts to look dry, dampen it again.

The first time you see a little spike of green popping out of the soil, you will feel such elation, especially if you have never grown anything before. You made this happen! You and water and earth and heat and clean air. Now the plant will reach for the sun, and as it grows, make sure you work hard towards your own intent. In doing so, you honour the earth and her gifts, and you in turn are inspired by the magic of the land.

Cleansing Flames

Some rather gory accounts from Geoffrey Keating's *History of Ireland* (c. 1634) describe how the druids in Munster lit the Fires of Tlachtgha (a powerful druidess, possibly even an ancient goddess, and daughter of Mog Roith), to burn human sacrifices in honour of the gods. This occurred on Samhain eve (October 31st at sunset) and all fires that night had to be lit from that flame, and those who disobeyed were fined. Fires are still lit annually at this time in Ireland, although as far as I know, no one is sacrificed upon them.

In the same chapter Keating also describes how at Beltane (or Bealltaine, as he writes it), cattle were driven through a fire to 'shield them from all diseases'. The more likely reason is that the heat would cause ticks to fall off, generally improving the health of the cattle.

So straight away we have a direct contradiction; fire used both to destroy and to heal. I think this is really important to take note of. All things are at least dual in nature, and indeed most things have many aspects. To say, for example, fire represents destruction is a massive over-simplification. When examining any aspect of magic or witchcraft, you have to understand that there are many different possibilities for every action. Certainly, every colour, herb, animal and even element has many correspondences, and the more you understand this, the deeper your understanding of witchcraft will become.

Fire can heal. Think of cauterising a wound, or of burning a field to leave it fertile for the next season. Fire can kill: that's an obvious one! But we do well to remember the power inherent here. Fire can be metaphorical; think about the fires of passion, the fires of creativity, the fire of anger. Fire destroys and fire creates. Metaphorically burning away that which is clogging up your life creates space for new and positive things to come to light.

An exercise a few of us sometimes do at Beltane is to write down, on a piece of paper, things we want to let go of. This can be emotion; perhaps an anger towards a friend who has let us down, or a sadness over a break up. It can also be something physical, like the reluctance to move house, or feeling stuck in your current job. We write the words and really think about why this situation or object is bothering us so much. Then we build a bonfire, as part of our Beltane celebrations, and once the flames are leaping high we throw the pieces of paper in and celebrate as they turn to ash. This is our sacrifice to the gods in a way. By doing this we make a commitment to our own soul that we will let this pain or difficulty go. We will move on, and become a richer and wiser person for doing so.

Another simple exercise demonstrates the calming and peaceful nature of fire. What! I hear you cry... Honestly, find a quiet, dim spot with no draughts and light a candle. Make yourself comfy and watch the flame. Watch how still it is, only moving slightly when the air from your own lungs disturbs it. Look at the amazing array of colours it holds. See how complex it is, but so simple too. Let your mind focus on the flame, and while your mind is busy doing all this you are letting go of worries, troubles and the bustle of the day. Your mind will relax, and in turn, so will your body.

Disclaimer: don't build fires unless you know what you are doing! And don't burn your house down with candles. Please. OK?

Finally, remember that in Celtic witchcraft, as in all things, everything is connected. Did you know that when a flame burns, it gives off gas and water? And smoke, of course, is tiny particles of burnt fuel, returning eventually to the earth. The world is complex and because of that, magic can be as complex or as simple as you want it to be. Don't limit yourself, keep your mind open to all possibilities, and feel the elements not only all around you, but within you as well.

Chapter 6

Wild Spirit

Celtic Triad: Three glories of a gathering: a comely mate, a good horse and a swift hound.

Animals and magic: it's an association as old as the hills. Modern media portrays the witch and her familiar; normally a cat, but often a bird, a toad or similar. Sadly, in the witch trials of the 16th and 17th centuries, it was normal for a close relationship with a cat or dog to be used against an alleged 'witch', with the accused often being tortured into admitting the animal was the devil in disguise, travelling from hell to aid with the malevolent magicks of the wicked one.

This idea, that the creature in question was only magical because of 'the devil', would likely have been ridiculed by the Celts. The Celts understood that animals had their own power in our world, and indeed in other worlds. Animals had powerful symbolism, were potent omens and were often the companions or even the hidden forms of gods and goddesses. If you read Celtic tales, you will have captured the sense that animals were viewed as powerful in their own right, opposing today's prevailing attitude, which seems to see animals only in light of how they benefit humankind; as pets, food or beasts of burden.

It seems to be one of the few universal aspects of the Pagans I have met that they all have a healthy respect for animals, and indeed a love and reverence for them that goes beyond the affection for a cute, cuddly pet. They (and I) respect the whole animal, even the grim, messy and gory bits that tend to get glossed over in pet shops. I'm going to tell you about a few animals that have held significance for me throughout my life. Some are prevalent in Celtic myth; others less so. But the key point is that the whole animal is respected as a significant and crucial part of our world and ecosystem. That is the Celtic way to look at animals.

The Crow

The reason the crow is my first port of call is I currently have one visiting. As I write this, we are approaching Imbolc, and in typical Pagan style my mum and dad are spring-cleaning. Yeah, okay, we live in England and it's nowhere near spring yet. In fact, I have just missed two days of work because the weather has disrupted travel that much. However, as a family we have always viewed Imbolc as the first stirrings of the earth; the wake-up call; the early warning system for the warmer months ahead. So, as my parents kick up dust and slap up wallpaper, it's not a great environment for Crowley, a rescue bird who is now about 17 years old. I found him injured as a fledgling, and we were told by the vet he would never fly and could never return to the wild. The vet suggested we'd be as well to put him down, as otherwise we would have to look after him for the rest of his life (which could be quite long; crows have been known to live longer than 50 years in captivity). Of course we accepted the task (gift) of looking after him, and now he's staying with me until the homestead becomes a little calmer.

Crowley is temperamental, noisy at times; confrontational, mischievous, playful and highly intelligent. Quite like the goddess he is most often linked to; The Morrígan.

In *The Wooing of Emer* we are told that Badb is the same as the Morrigu (The Morrígan) and that she is the battle crow and a goddess of battle. The word Badb, or Badhbh (pronounced something akin to Bayve) actually means crow, and Badb the goddess is also named Badb Catha, the battle crow. The similarities between the goddess(es) and the bird include the dark shadows they throw over the battlefield, the wailing cries and the stubborn and wilful nature they both seem to have. Being associated with battle seems to naturally tie in associations with death, which makes sense as the crow is a scavenger; a carrion eater, and a battlefield for a crow is basically an all-you-can-eat buffet with extra juicy bits.

Bresal, King of the Formorians, named his druid 'Crow', for being wry, witty with words and greedy (*The Metrical Dindshenchas*). I've never known Crowley to be particularly greedy, but he is savvy. If he is full, sometimes he will take the piece of food I am proffering and hide it away somewhere. Later, I will see him sidle back to his stash and, spying suspiciously around to make sure he is not spotted, he will surreptitiously slide his treasure out for a sneaky snack.

Crows can learn to speak, but even without this talent they are fantastic communicators. Today, he was sitting on his perch and I took his fresh water and food to him. I passed him the water bowl and held it while he had a sip, then put it on the ground below him. I did the same with the food bowl, but he wasn't hungry at that moment. Instead of ignoring it as many animals would, he tapped the rim of the bowl then pointed at the ground with his beak. I put the dish where he pointed and he was happy.

Through the telling of old Celtic tales and simple observations we can tie the following correspondences and attributes to the crow:

- Badb
- Morrígan
- Nemain
- Battlefields, the start or end of battle, the aftermath, the oncoming storm
- Wit
- Intellect
- Communication
- Death

- Change
- Moving between worlds
- Mischief
- Devotion (crows mate for life)
- Stubbornness, wilfulness

So as a witch, how does this help you? Well, if you are meditating, and the image of a crow appears, perhaps the above correspondences may help you decide what the meaning of that is. The same for omens; perhaps a crow flies into your path, or watches you from a nearby building. If you are creating a spell pouch to give you confidence in an interview, perhaps the small image of a crow in the pouch could boost your faith in your communication skills; give you the gift of the gab.

The crow is by no means the only corvid with magical associations; it is simply the one with which I have most experience. There are far more people with friendly ravens, widely considered a much more intelligent bird. Then there's the rook, a noisy animal that builds large communities. The thieving magpie is a beautiful orca of the avian world, shiny and raucous, but feared by blackbirds and thrushes for its attacks on nests. And you haven't seen cheekiness personified until you've seen jackdaws strutting bold as you like across the rocks of Brimham, picking up scraps yet acting like no human ever set foot there.

I hope someday to delve further into the world of corvids and their magical significance, but I can certainly say that as well as being a wonderful companion, a crow is a diverse and useful magical symbol, and the creature itself exudes a sense of other-worldliness – perhaps only because of its incredible intelligence combined with being so alien to ourselves.

The Dog

Yes, I am going for the obvious Celtic animal here, and why not? I touched on them briefly in *A Modern Celt*, but here I have the time and space to get a bit more into the nitty gritty and explore these associations more deeply.

The Hound is a phrase that instantly becomes a title in Celtic legend mainly because of Cú Chulainn. He is 'The Hound of Ulster' and with that phrase he tells us the hound or dog is respected as being fierce, brave and loyal; as he is himself. This also tells us that the dog is dangerous, unpredictable and won't always come to heel.

For any of you who have experience with dogs, the above should surely ring true. Dogs are fantastic animals, but all too often people forget to respect these powerful carnivores, and it's sad that ill-trained dogs or even abused dogs can become violent and aggressive animals. However, a well-loved, well-treated dog will be the most wonderful companion you could imagine. Again, it's all about respecting the animal exactly as you would respect a person. You wouldn't expect a child to behave to your standards without any guidance. You certainly wouldn't expect it to be well balanced and happy without love, affection and the other basics of life such as food, warmth and shelter.

So why, as a society, are we always shocked when abused or neglected animals become vicious? And why do we tend to blame the animal, rather than the humans responsible? It's completely illogical behaviour. Humans domesticated dogs; they are not wild animals. They rely on the relationships with humans just as we rely on them. Yet somehow, probably because of twisted media coverage and sheer ignorance, we have this idea that certain breeds of dog are inherently nasty, stupid or aggressive. It's simply not the case. I have known pit bulls, Rottweilers, Dobermans and other breeds 'known' for their 'poor temperament'. They have all been wonderful animals, because they were cared for properly, loved and treated with respect.

As a Celtic witch, it's so important that you learn to avoid knee-jerk reactions to stressful situations, and with animals you must always look at the whole picture. Is it the dog that is at fault, or the owner? You must look, and make your own decision. A dog can also be a great judge of character, so if your dog is normally friendly, but their hackles rise at a particular person, maybe you should be a little more cautious with that person!

The dog is:

- Courageous
- Loving
- A symbol of hearth and home
- A symbol of hunting
- Loyal
- Fierce
- Caring
- A sign of order or of a situation becoming less chaotic
- A white dog is a messenger from the underworld
- Jealous
- Vicious
- Carefree
- Fun
- Simple pleasures, joy
- Companionable
- A sign of a partnership or team
- Protective
- The symbol of Cú Chulainn and also associated with Lugh

Dogs are so easy to observe that you could add and add to this list, but the above correspondences are the main ones that come to mind for me.

Close your eyes; imagine you are the dog. You are running; not from anything, not towards anything. You simply run for the joy; to feel the earth pounding beneath your padded feet, like a great, green heartbeat; to feel the air rushing through your hair and drying out your lolling tongue as you take great gasps of it. You are unfettered pleasure; you are speed and grace and power and you are not purposeless; your purpose is to be this way and revel in being who you are. Capture this feeling, and keep it with you as you open your eyes. You are perfect, just the way you are. Take pleasure in it.

The Bee

Another animal that has had many sacred associations throughout the aeons, yet is mentioned all too infrequently in Celtic texts. We know the Celts ate honey and drank mead, so they must have had skill with bees, yet it is rarely written of by the scholars of the Middle Ages who gave us most of the Celtic literature we now refer to.

The bee is another dangerous animal that simply needs to be respected. Yes, a bee can sting you and undoubtedly it will hurt. It can even kill, if you are sensitive or allergic to the venom. However, the reasons for a bee to sting you are so few and far between, that the threat is far less than it initially appears.

Bees form hives; great, thriving communities where everyone knows their place. It's hardly utopian; there can be violent disputes within a hive! But bees work together and are even considered to have a 'hive mind', where everyone knows what needs to be done without being told, and all work together seamlessly.

My mum and dad always had (and still have) a garden full of the kind of flowers that attract bees and butterflies; buddleia, honesty, hebe, poppies and more. Occasionally we would find a fat, stripy bee stunned where it had flown too vigorously near a door or window. I would pick the poor creature up, its soft coat like velvet beneath my careful fingers. I would put it on a plate near a tiny pool of sugar water. The bee, once it had regained consciousness, would crawl to the sugar water and lap it up with its proboscis. Fascinated, I would watch the tiny straw curl in and out of the bee's mouth like a miniature party whistle. Once recovered, the bee would simply fly off and return to the industrious examination of every flower in sight.

I never felt worried or scared by the bees. They had a job to do, and as long as I wasn't stopping them, or threatening their hive, I didn't even register them as anything but part of the background.

The bee is, ultimately, one tiny part of an incredible, living machine. Just like one of your internal organs, or a cell. Of course, some bees are solitary, so I am generalising somewhat, but as a symbol for working together, systems, order and industry, few animals work as well as bees. Perhaps ants, but I have little experience with ants, so bees it is for me!

Bees represent:

- Industry
- Productivity
- Focus
- Teamwork
- Order
- Matriarchy
- Nourishment
- Family
- Fastidiousness
- Community
- Hidden danger
- Open communication
- Empathy
- Avoiding selfishness
- Putting others first
- Organisation
- Growth (perhaps of an idea or project)

If you have a garden, find out what plants you can grow in your local area that will attract bees. These will depend on the type of soil you have and whether your garden is in sun or shade, so do a bit of research and with a little effort you should have bees visiting every spring and summer.

Bees are a vital part of our ecosystem and account for a huge percentage of pollination of crops worldwide. In the US, colonies of bees are rented by farms to aid with pollination. About three million colonies are rented each year. This doesn't even include all the wild bees that naturally pollinate whatever they can as part and parcel of their everyday routine. However, for the past eight years or more, a phenomenon called Colony Collapse Disorder – the failure of hives and the subsequent death of billions of bees – has been closely linked to multiple fungicides and pesticides, most notably but not solely the infamous neonicotinoids. If the bees die, we die – simple as that. Anything you can do to encourage bees and organic farming that avoids the use of these chemicals will ultimately benefit the whole world, particularly humankind.

So add to the list of correspondences 'cause and effect', and the humbling fact that the tiniest animal really can hold the key to the survival of an entire species; many species in fact.

You will, no doubt, have your own favourite animals, and as stated previously, it really doesn't matter if the animal has 'Celtic roots' or not; the Celt is in the way you view the animal, the way you interact with it, the respect you give it, and the ability to see it as a vital part of the world. Search for the magic it brings us; whether that be joy, the ability to focus on a spell, or a correspondence that allows you to analyse a situation or perhaps see into the future somewhat.

Understanding animals helps us understand ourselves. They are no less complex than us 'human animals', but they are less arrogant, and can teach us not only to not take ourselves so seriously, but also to not take our place at the top of the food chain for granted.

Next time you eat meat, give thanks to the animal that gave it to you. Think about where it came from, and the life it led before it came to your plate.

Next time you are in a pet shop that stocks live animals, stop and observe the animals' behaviour. If the animals are well looked after, praise the shopkeeper. Those who respect animals should be rewarded.

Next time you witness animal cruelty, speak up or take action in a way that won't put you in danger. Please don't try to break up a dog fight or anything that may get you injured! Instead, contact your local authorities and find out what you can do to make a difference.

Every act of kindness is a powerful magic and a commitment you make to your own soul to be a better person; a better witch. Look to the animal kingdom to see how nurturing and kindness exists outside words and rooftops, and be amazed and humbled by it.

Chapter 7

Between Cauldron and Club

Celtic Triad: There are three things that are never at rest in anyone: the heart in working, the breath in moving, and the soul in purposing.

Every witch has their tools. Some may have shelves filled with crystals, ornaments and herbs. Some may have nothing but a piece of clothing that has been cleansed and consecrated, or a sacred space. I have a sacred space I have created in my mind, where I can go to wherever I am. When I travel, I can go here even if the only place I have to work or meditate is a hotel room, or more usually, a tent! We each have our own way of working. Whether you are a magical minimalist or a hoarder of arcane artefacts, you can thank your Celtic forebears for many of the occult tools we naturally reach for in the modern age.

As well as physical tools, it's important to remember we have the tools of skill, wisdom and craft; the knowledge and secrets that we use to create magic; to manifest our intent.

The Cauldron

Ah, the archetypal image of the crone hunched over a bubbling cauldron, stirring and muttering foul curses as evil magicks fill the air. Although this stereotype is hilarious in its inaccuracy, there is (as in most tales) some truth behind the magic of the cauldron, and much of that magic is told in tales handed down from or inspired by the Celts.

The Gundestrup Cauldron is a real, almost pure silver cauldron that was discovered in 1891. It is thought to hail from the 1st or 2nd century BC, and although there is some dispute over its origins, it is widely accepted that this is a European

Celtic, Iron Age piece of work. The vessel is decorated with torques, musical instruments, animals, plants and a horned god that could be Cernnunos. So it's not hard to draw the conclusion that cauldrons were important enough not only to use a vast amount of precious metal on, but to be decorated with sacred symbols and pictures.

One of the most famous cauldrons from Celtic inspired literature is the Dagda's cauldron of plenty. 'No company would go from it unsatisfied' *The Book of Invasions* (compiled 11th century CE) tells us, indicating an endless feast, but one that was fairly divided between the guests waiting to eat. No-one was given too much, or too little, so we can see this as a symbol also of balance, fairness and even justice. The cauldron here is also a physical representation of hospitality. The Celts held hospitality in great regard; it was most frowned upon to either refuse or deny hospitality. The idea of a cauldron providing unending food is probably the root of the leprechaun's cauldron of endless gold. Riches mean different things to different people.

In Welsh tradition, the Cauldron of Dyrnwch the Giant is one of the Thirteen Treasures of Great Britain. This cauldron is again a cooking vessel, but this time will only cook well and quickly for a brave man, and if a coward tries to cook with the cauldron his meat will not boil.

For the modern witch, a cauldron is often a symbol of femininity, the bowl representing the womb or belly, and the opening representing the vagina. It is the ultimate symbol of birth and rebirth, and as such is often used ritually as an earth symbol. The earth is constantly renewing and changing, and we associate the earth with a mother goddess more than any other element.

The cauldron has a rich and complex history and I am sad to merely skim the surface for you. To sum up, the cauldron may be used for:

- Representing earth
- Burning incense (earth into air, protection, transformation, the combination of elements)
- A symbol of hospitality/home and hearth
- A symbol of wealth of spirit i.e. not material riches but food, shelter, love, spirituality etc
- A symbol of womanhood
- New beginnings
- Scrying
- Potion making (real or metaphorical)
- Cooking (obviously!)
- As a ritual vessel for drink, say for brags or toasts at a seasonal gathering

The list really does go on and on. The cauldron is a versatile, practical tool with an incredible, magical heritage. You can nearly always find a 'crafty' use for it.

I have in the past used a small one to burn things that were of no use to me anymore; that were holding me back. The fire ate my words on the pieces of earth (paper) that I wrote them on. The fire and earth created water (it does, look it up; science!) and drifted away to the air. I was reborn in that cauldron, my past drifting away on a cocktail of elements, while the cauldron, empty again, allowed me to move on unfettered.

Erynn Rowan Laurie speaks of three internal cauldrons as originally described by the fili (sacred poet) Amirgen White. (*Cauldron of Poesy*, circa 7th century, text 16th century). You can imagine your mind, body and soul as three cauldrons, each filled to a certain level and constantly tipping and spilling, yet also constantly being refilled by your own actions and thoughts, and particularly your emotions. The poem in the ancient text tells us the cauldrons are particularly moved by sorrow and joy.

This is very typical of the Celts. Modern spiritual teachers often suggest we should never focus on the negative; in fact we should try to banish negativity of any kind. The Celts accepted that bad times and hardship were a part of life, and used those experiences to grow, change and become stronger. As a Celtic witch, you must never deny your anger, your sorrow, your jealousy or your fear. You must embrace them; let them tip your internal cauldrons and feel how those emotions affect you. Then take action to restore the balance. Move away from the stressful situation; lose the friend who angers you; vent your frustration at the gym or on a video game; play your musical instrument until the roof lifts with the energy created by your rage. A Celtic witch does not deny those emotions some see as negative; a Celtic witch uses them to their advantage.

Music

Which brings us nicely to my favourite Celtic tool: music. Music is, of course, not a physical thing you can pick up and wield, but it is an amazing magical tool. Before you scoff at this, at how simple music, found everywhere, can be magical, think about the last time a song made you cry; the last time you tapped your foot, clapped your hands or bopped your head in time to a catchy beat; the last time you were angry and a song helped you vent that anger and release the pressure. Now tell me music isn't magical.

Music is one of the greatest therapies we have, and a universal communication tool. You can listen to songs from anywhere in the world, regardless of language, and get a sense of the emotion conveyed by the melody. It's the music itself that carries the message that goes beyond words.

This is why music is wonderful for communicating with other worlds; the worlds beyond what we can see, and just as important, the hidden worlds within ourselves. We all have parts of ourselves we cannot access, or don't want to see. Music helps break down subconscious walls and allows us to move freely within our soul.

Think of relaxing music during meditation, or a chant that

gathers the energy within a circle. Think of thousands of voices raised in song, or a lone soloist whose voice rings true and clear through a silent auditorium. Music has the power to raise the hairs on the back of your neck and give you goose-bumps. It manipulates our emotions and even affects us physically – a deep, bass note can have a peculiar effect on our bowels, for example!

The obvious question here is: 'But what if I don't play music?' Good question. Relevant question! The answer is: you do. You really do. Even if all you do is slap your hands together in joy, or mimic bird song, or hum tunelessly, you will, absolutely, do something that is musical.

The common fall-back for those magicians who find that melody is beyond them, is the drum. To create a beat, a rhythm, is quite something. If you find you are struggling to find rhythm, look within; listen to your heartbeat. Hear how it keeps its own time; hear how it changes in tune with your emotions and state of mind. Feel how it slows as you relax and unwind. Try to emulate this beat on the drum, any drum, or even on your own knees or a table. You may think you have no musical talent, but you are rhythm incarnate, and you can externalise this with the power of your own mind and body.

An Exercise for Letting Go

Visualise something you want to be rid of; an emotion, a situation, a bad habit; anything at all. Crouch on the floor as if ready to spring up. Pitch your voice as low as it will go; it is deep, like the deep-rooted invader you are wishing to expel. Make a sound you are comfortable with, like ahhhhhh or ohhhhhhh. Rise slowly from the floor, and as you do, let the pitch of your voice become higher and louder. All the while visualise the thing you want to be rid of being plucked from your life and banished. Continue to rise, physically and in tone, until you are standing, arms to the air, shouting at the top of your voice! Perhaps this is one to do when your neighbours are out. You will feel refreshed, invigorated and empowered.

Music can be used in many ways in your witchcraft. For example, a bell is often used in group magic to signal a moment of transformation. In guided meditation, it may be used to help the meditators reach the mind state they are trying to achieve. Singing ritual words instead of speaking them may reinforce their effect for a particular spell. A sad melody or joyful tune will completely change the impact of your work.

The Dagda's harp, sometimes named Daurdabla, the oak of two greens, was famous for playing the three noble strains of Ireland: geantrai, joyous music; goltrai, the lament and finally suantrai, the music of sleep. Men would fall about laughing as if drunk when the geantrai was heard, then cry uncontrollably when the goltrai took hold. No-one could withstand the soothing strains of the suantrai, and soldiers would drop to the ground where they stood, fast asleep.

This legend is important because it shows us the sheer power the Celts believed music holds. The wonderful thing is that power has not changed or diminished through the ages. Music is a universal constant. As long as birds can sing, and waves can crash against the shore, and wind can whisper through the trees, the world is playing its symphony to you. Don't be afraid to join in.

Binding

Binding can mean the physical binding of an object or person, just as Cú Chulainn was bound to the rock to await his death. Or it can mean the metaphorical binding to a quest, a geas, or an obligation. Again thinking of Cú Chulainn, he was bound not to eat dog meat and also to not refuse hospitality. The conflict of these two geas were his downfall.

Words have power, as we will explore further in the next chapter. Make sure your word is binding. Never break your promises. Never promise something you cannot achieve. Never do something you are forbidden to do – normally by yourself! Likewise, don't forbid yourself do to things unreasonably. Don't set yourself unrealistic goals.

Returning to the *Cauldron of Poesy*, Laurie explains that the virtue of preserving (or delaying as it is sometimes translated as), refers either to a binding spell; literally preserving things the way they are by binding the situation; or judicial binding, where a person is bound to appear before a judge or court. She also muses that there is a binding between prosecutor and accused that cannot be broken, and lasts until litigation is complete.

You can use the same point of view when you are performing magic for another. You have an unseen connection to that person until the spell is complete and all effects have passed. Viewing magic in this way encourages you to be careful; if you rush, or are lazy, or have twisted intent towards your 'client', this will affect you just as much as it does them. You are bound to them by your own intent to transform their world in some way. Depending on the intent, this bind may last forever! So be careful what you promise to do and who for.

I've already spoken in an earlier chapter about binding your intent up in cords and plaiting them to keep the intent held within. You can do many different spells in a similar way. The best time for binding spells is at the dark moon, when the blackness encourages us to be more introspective and look deeper within ourselves to the root of our intent. The moon no longer reflects the sun; she is only herself, dark and true. You must be as the dark moon, reflecting no-one's desires but your own.

You can visualise a tricky situation as you tie a false knot in a cord, ribbon or rope. Then imagine the situation unravelling as you tug the rope, watching the knot disappear. See how simply the problems fall away. Feel your mind start to unravel as you apply yourself to the problem with new clarity.

Take a piece of paper and write on it something you wish to bind away from yourself; something you wish to keep clear of you. This may be a person, an emotion or a situation. Using a clean, new cord, tie the paper to a rock, criss-crossing the cord over and over until the paper is literally bound to the rock with no way to escape. Take the rock far away from your home and bury it.

A week long series of meditations can be marked off by tying a knot in a piece of cord each time you leave the meditative state. At the end of the week, sit and hold the cord, think about how committed you were. Each knot is a symbol of your work, your magic; your mental discipline. You may keep the cord on your altar, to remind you of what you can achieve, or you may bury or burn (carefully!) the cord, to send the magic you have done away with the elements.

The Club

As well as his great cauldron of plenty, the Dagda was also famous for his club. The club is, in part, the counterpart to the cauldron's femininity. The phallic symbolism is obvious! This club was said to slay nine men in one swing, yet the handle could return the dead to life.

Just as the cauldron is a symbol of birth and rebirth, the club here is a symbol of the cycle of life. Things die; things are reborn. Without this, there is no balance. The club is also a tool for reaching between worlds. The handle, in your hand, represents you, rooted in this world. The rest of the club is reaching into the world of the aos sí (literally, people of the mounds, referring to the fae who live inside the hollow hills), the world we cannot see, in order to manipulate energies and manifest your will. This represents your mind and spirit, reaching beyond your physical body.

A club may seem a little unwieldy to some, so you can substitute the more obvious wand or staff while retaining the same meaning or power. You can even visualise your intent while simply gesturing with your finger or whole hand. The important thing to remember is the club represents balance and the circular nature of life; cause and effect. Be mindful of the consequences of your actions; how they affect others, how they affect yourself and how they may affect you in the future. Be willing to take responsibility for your actions. You wield the power and therefore you have to clean up any messes you make!

In Celtic legend, the Dagda's own son, Cermait, scolds his dad for being a bit trigger-happy with the club (or staff, as it is in this tale). Cermait wants to know why his dad has killed three men just because he could. The Dagda is ashamed, and brings the men back to life. The Dagda was lucky to have a loving family member, who understood his magic and was willing to point his mistake out to him.

Sadly, I know we don't all have that luxury, and many of you may work entirely alone at times. This is why it is so important that you are honest with yourself about your reasons for doing magic. You may be the only person who can point out your mistakes to yourself. Don't be afraid to do this; never shy away from your responsibilities, always do your best to repair mistakes and be prepared to laugh at yourself when things go wrong. If you can laugh, then you will never be bitter. If you avoid bitterness, you avoid resentment. If you avoid resentment, you free your mind and spirit to journey to worlds beyond what we see now; worlds far away and worlds deep within ourselves.

Chapter 8

Splendid Poison

Celtic Triad: Three occasions for one to speak falsehood without excuse: to save the life of one who is innocent, to keep the peace among neighbours, and to preserve the Wise and their crafts.

Celtic tales only come to us courtesy of the scholars of the Middle Ages, who were proud of their manuscripts and the ability to write and illuminate these beautiful, treasured documents. Writing, in the Middle Ages, was a coveted skill; not something to be taken for granted, as many of us do today.

In contrast, the Celts barely wrote anything down. There are a few scratchings of Ogham here and there, but for the most part, the written word was alien to them. This may seem to go against the supposition, nay the fact, that words were seen as enormously powerful by the Celts. Satirist, poets and bards were revered and respected, even held in awe. A well-known satirist would be accepted into any king's court at a minute's notice, because the ruler feared the acid bite of the wordsmith's tongue, and the damage it could to his reputation and that of his household. It was thought that a well-spoken satire would cause blemishes to appear on the victim's skin, as an outward represen-tation of the alleged corruption within.

If anything, the lack of Celtic writing supports their respect for words. Words spoken can never be taken back, but the written word may be destroyed; it may be altered, or hidden, or denied. The spoken word is the ultimate weapon as long as there are ears to hear it. A poet may move a room to tears, and this is magic of the moment. Reading that poem at home later is unlikely to have quite the same effect. A sly word in the ear of a gossip may spread a malicious rumour all around town, and who is to say where it originated? Words are powerful, and while you are able to (and encouraged to) write your own words down, it is important you learn to respect the awesome effect words can have on other people, the universe and of course, yourself.

Poetry

Poetry is a love of mine; more than a hobby, more than a diversion and more than simply stringing words together. Every year I participate in NaPoWriMo, which is the challenge to write a poem a day for a month. Each poem must be entirely new. Making this kind of commitment to yourself is very focusing, and writing poetry in this way prompts you to be aware of everything around you. Searching for inspiration is mindfulness itself; exploring how things are, right now, and recording them with the written word in a form that will entertain others.

Poetry is not just about clever form and rhyming schemes. Poetry is about telling stories; using the rhythm of words to play your point into the reader or listener's mind. Poetry is about the musicality of language. Poetry is about emotion; love and loathing; pain and regret; joy and anticipation. Poetry is a vehicle for feelings, hopes and dreams. The Gaelic word that was used for Celtic poets was 'file' (or 'fili'), which literally means 'one who sees'. A good poet sees all, and uses what they see to enchant and amuse others.

I and Pangur Bán my cat,
'Tis a like task we are at:
Hunting mice is his delight,
Hunting words I sit all night.
Better far than praise of men
'Tis to sit with book and pen;
Pangur bears me no ill-will,
He too plies his simple skill.

This extract from Pangur Bán, a poem by an anonymous Irish monk from the 9th century CE, likens his cat's hunt for mice to the writer's own hunt for words. The mice are elusive, but the delight in capturing them is beyond measure. Poetry is like this. The struggle to find the words that will evoke the exact emotion you are feeling is hard, strenuous, maddening; but the completed poem is so pleasurable, every moment of the struggle is a joy.

Poetry is also very cathartic. Pent-up emotions can be bad for us, can even lead to physical problems such as ulcers, headaches and high blood pressure, and of course a multitude of mental health problems. Poetry gives us a very real outlet for the words we might not be able to say out loud to someone else. It can take us on a journey of recovery or self-discovery. It can be our punching bag, our pillow to cry into and our best friend when we are all alone. Letting someone else read your poetry is a great intimacy, so it can even be helpful in personal relationships or bring you closer to a family member.

But what if you've never written before? Well, the best answer to that is to think about what you want to write about, and to read some poetry on that subject. Google 'poems about...' and read as many as you can get your hands on. Record the names of poets that inspire you. Examine how the poet strings words together. Do they use rhyme? Is it just a stream of consciousness? Make notes, mental or physical, and try to emulate the style of a writer that resonates with you. Remember, no one is marking you on this. Your poetry is a magic for you and you alone.

Try writing down a list of words that pop up while you are dwelling on your chosen subject. For 'bees' you might have: honey, flowers, pollen, work, joy, summer. Form a sentence around each of those words. Now put those sentences into an order that pleases you. Try reading it out aloud; maybe even record it and play it back to yourself. How does it sound? Change it until you are happy with it. Don't be afraid to edit ruthlessly, but also don't be afraid to think: 'This is good enough,' and leave it as it is.

When you have finished your poem, keep it somewhere safe. If you are able and confident enough, keep it on show somewhere so you can be proud of your work. You have just externalised some of your feelings, and used them to create something new in this world. Feel the confidence that washes through you; feel that any negative emotions are diminished by this process, and that positive ones are lifted and highlighted by the power of your words. Poetry is a magic that will never end; as long as we have words, we will weave them and give them to each other.

Spells

After reading about the power of poetry, it should come as no surprise that many magical rituals are written in a poetic style. Think of most spells you have seen written down, from any path. Nearly all of them will be in a form of verse. This is because the rhythm of the words helps to focus your mind on the task at hand. This frees up the rest of your mind to channel the magic, or energy required for your spell.

Now Lugh rests his shining head
Now the call to those called 'Dead'
The cavalcade of fairy folk
Cernunnos in his winter cloak
Who calls to beasts; the stag, the hound
Who calls the great hunt, starts the sound
Of hooves a-drumming on the ground
Hide so you won't be found!
The green that rests within the oak
The holly still in winter's choke
Frantic, bursting to be free
Herne rides the land and sea.
Great lord, great god, great grasping hand

That holds the seasons, holds the land
And holds the reins: the hunt so wild
And every adult, every child
Will know he is abroad this night
As wild wind whips the world in fright
And the Sun stands still.

This is an excerpt from a Winter Solstice ritual I penned a few years ago. The purpose of this section was to focus the male energy in the room and evoke the presence of the male god; the Holly King, Cernunnos or the Green Man: the energy of the forest that goes by many names. The rhythm of the words kept all of us focused on the theme and the intent of the work, and as the pace of the reading increased, so did the energy in the room increase.

Spellcraft is all about transformation, as what we are doing when we cast a spell is hoping to change something within our universe. Words are incredibly evocative, and with the skill of a poet, you can use your words to mesmerise and enchant, focus and drive, predict and prophesy, calm and soothe, confuse and befuddle, impassion and allure.

You can also use the shapes of words as well as their rhythm to create magic. Each letter of a word can become the first letter of the line of a spell. Written down, this can intensify your intent and focus your energy more specifically.

Heal my friend and make her well
Ease her pain with my kind spell
Aid her now to health and light
Let her feel the sun so bright.

This is a very simple little rhyme where the capital letters on the left hand side read **HEAL**. Chanted over and over, the word 'heal' becomes the subconscious and conscious focus of the practitioner, making it the undisputed focus of this spell.

In Irish literature, spells and magic are used for transformations, shape-changing, cursing, sleep, healing and prophecy. Mogh Roith, the blind druid of Munster, used his words to control the weather and put fear into the hearts of his enemies.

I cast a spell,
on the power of cloud,
may there be a rain
of blood on grass,
let it be throughout the land,
a burning of the crowd,
may there be a trembling
on the warriors of Conn.
(Excerpt from *The Siege of Knocklong*, circa 15th century CE, translation copyright Seán Ó Duinn, 1992)

There is a sort of calm viciousness to these words, a sense that the fury of the druid is being focused fully into these words. The words themselves are well thought out, sparse and undecorated. They speak the druid's intent and nothing more. There is no room for misinterpretation.

In your own magic, you should always make sure your intent is clear. Your words are a fantastic tool to do this. Wiccans (and others) use the phrase 'an it harm none' meaning 'as long as nobody gets hurt'. This phrase is often used as a disclaimer in spell or ritual, to ensure that no 'monkey's paw' situation arises; the magic will occur without detriment to anyone. The only danger with such a readily repeatable phrase as this is it can become stated by habit rather than with intent, thus losing its protective power. This is why your own words are so powerful, because they come from a place deep within you, and carry your magic out into the world.

Song

Brigid, who is also known as Persephone
Rises like an epiphany
From the womb of winter's death.

These are the opening lines to a song I wrote while walking home just before Imbolc about ten years ago. I was in a very suburban setting, houses and pavements and telegraph poles, but the sun was milky white in a hazy blue sky, and the January chill was offset by a warming sense of the approaching spring. There were blackbirds, Lon Dubh, calling and shouting, and even a wren chattering angrily as I invaded its territory. I remember feeling overcome with joy and gratitude that I could be a part of this burst of life, and I started humming. The tune was quickly recorded onto my phone, and later it became a full song that spoke of the world awakening after winter, both outside and within yourself. You can hear the song here: https://sound cloud.com/mabh-savage/brigid-2012.

This burst of inspiration is often called Awen by the druids, and trust me, it is an elusive but wonderful feeling. Even songs I am particularly proud of have not stemmed from true Awen, but from everyday occurrences, emotional epiphany or often, simple hard graft. Awen does not come when called, indeed, if anything, it calls to you. Thankfully, there is plenty of inspiration in everyday life for even the most jaded of songwriters!

In the last chapter we examined the use of music as a magical tool, in particular drumming and chanting. I appreciate that not everyone who reads this will be able to compose and write a song, but if you can appreciate the form within poetry, and the magic within the words of a spell, then you can understand and revel in the sorcery of song.

I've often been at a group ritual where the leader bursts into song, often something quite simple such as the chant Earth my Body, so that others can join in if they wish. The sudden transformation either from spoken word or simple silence to entrancing music is a beautiful shock to the system. It lifts our souls and literally, physically moves our minds onto a different plane. Brainwaves can be affected in various ways by audio stimulus, particularly music. Relaxing music increases the frequency of alpha waves, which is the same increase seen when moving into a meditative state. Increasing the alpha wave frequency normally lowers the frequency and amplitude of the ever-present beta waves, which reduces stress, anxiety and tension.

So the magic of song is not just a thing of legend, but a widely documented scientific fact. Maybe the Dagda's harp did put folks to sleep, by over-stimulating their brains and inducing a theta wave state just like that of a dream.

Think of a song that means something to you. Why is it important? Is it the tune or the words? Where were you when you first heard this song? What was happening? How did you feel? How does hearing it make you feel now? Do you associate this song with any one person in particular? Do you share this song with others or listen to it alone? Does it evoke a particular smell or vision? Write these thoughts down and I think you will be surprised at just how much one song can affect you.

I remember listening to the album Physical Graffiti by Led Zeppelin when I was very young, just a child. I used to take my Walkman to bed with me and fall asleep listening to In the Light. Even now, that song still makes me think of late summer evenings, drifting off with the first touches of my dream world flickering around my eyelids. The haunting opening notes combined with the soaring vocal never fail to lift my spirits, and because I have enjoyed that song all through growing up, it feels timeless to me, like it can transport me back to any moment in my past that I care to explore.

Now that I write songs and perform them for others, I do try to make them as magical as possible, both in lyric and melody, but it is incredibly difficult to pour yourself wholeheartedly into every single piece. Some songs are already alive and just waiting for you to pluck them from the ether. These ones flow and tease then blossom under the gentlest of care. Others lurk in the darkness, refusing to be finished and hiding their hooks and riffs in great, frustrating shadows. Being a bard in the musical sense is both a great joy and an endless struggle, and as such is rewarding and exhausting in equal measure.

A bard in druidic terms is also a keeper of history; a teller of tales. The British Druidic Order tells us that: 'The central principle of the bardic path is communication, chiefly through word and sound.'

Osborn Bergin, in his 1970 piece Irish Bardic Poetry, quotes a lecture from 1912:

> For we must remember that the Irish file or bard was not necessarily an inspired poet. That he could not help. He was, in fact, a professor of literature and a man of letters, highly trained in the use of a polished literary medium, belonging to a hereditary caste in an aristocratic society, holding an official position therein by virtue of his training, his learning, his knowledge of the history and traditions of his country and his clan. He discharged, as O'Donovan pointed out many years ago, the functions of the modern journalist. He was not a song writer. He was often a public official, a chronicler, a political essayist, a keen and satirical observer of his fellow-countrymen.

So as a songwriter, is it our responsibility to observe and tell the tales of the world around us? I would say that's certainly true for folk musicians, but most modern pop music strays far from this path. Of course, that makes the magical music stand out all the more sharply, so perhaps this is no bad thing. My only concern is that as a society we have lost reverence for the true art of song, as it is so readily available in a canned, commercial variety that has lost so much of its original mystery and wonder.

Hopefully, after reading about poetry, spells and songs you have a more respectful attitude towards your own words. Perhaps as you write your journals, you will think about the words you jot down, and perhaps try to order some of your magical experiences into verse that will remind you of the day later? Or perhaps you will simply be more careful and wise in your choice of words to others, understanding that words, once spoken, can never be taken back.

As we move towards the end of this volume, it should be clear that every chapter emphasises the need for personal responsibility. Your words are your power made manifest; do not abuse that power, and do not let others do the same to you.

Chapter 9

Highway under the Hills

Celtic Triad: Three unbreathing things paid for only with breathing things: an apple tree, a hazel bush, a sacred grove.

I decided to head this final chapter with the above triad as it speaks to me firstly of mystery. Witchcraft is, at its heart, a mysterious skill; a mystical undertaking that is understood by few. Harnessing magic from within yourself and from the wider universe is a challenge and an art and as such, cannot be fathomed by those who see only the mundane.

Secondly, it tells me of our responsibility towards other living things. We pay for the unbreathing things (although to me, trees and groves do breathe and thrive) with our time and our respect; we must honour the world around us and be truly a part of it if we want to find divinity. We cannot take the natural world for granted. We must nourish it where we can, repair it when needed and always be grateful for the gifts it gives us.

Finally, it reminds me of the power of words. A short sentence can evoke the most complex of thoughts, and that is an important lesson to understand in any magical undertaking.

In this short introduction to Celtic witchcraft we have examined using the connection to our ancestors to reach into both the past and future, and to be mindful of ourselves in the moment. We have seen how we can honour the ancient while remaining thoroughly modern. We have discovered stepping stones across a great river, and how to light our own candles to see through the darkness or fog that may shadow our path. We have learned how to tell the turning of the months by only the moon, and enjoy the seasons through the weather and the changing colours that surround us. We have seen how each of these colours has a magical significance, and how you can observe, understand, and work these into your craft. We've looked to the elements, and how to harness them. We've spoken with feather and fur, and learned to appreciate all forms of life, even those we may have found unsavoury before. We've seen how many different tools can be employed in witchcraft, but that the most important tools are your mind and heart. Most recently, we walked through a web of words; of songs, spells and poetry, finding rhythms and rhymes that will focus and magnify our intent.

So what now? What is left to learn on this path of the Celtic witch? It should come as no surprise that there are many things to learn, and unless reading this is only a refresher for you, you will probably be only one or two steps across that great river. How you reach the other side is entirely up to you, but here are some thoughts from someone who of course, as yet, has not reached the other side herself.

Write Everything Down

I cannot overstate the importance of keeping a notebook. I said right at the start of this book that you would need one, and as you come close to finishing this book you will need it more than ever. Other people's books (mine included) are good points of reference, but your own experiences are unique. There will be times when you want to remember a particular spell, or chant, or feeling, or where you were when you saw a pair of red kites dancing overhead. Your journal should be something you can pick up and refer back to anytime you need to refresh your memory or even just to remind yourself why you are on this path. Write notes, draw sketches, dry flowers, record recipes; whatever is important to you should be in that journal. Make it personal to you, keep it safe and only share it with those you trust implicitly. It is your guide and your friend. It is a part of you that is committed to paper, and that is sacred magic indeed.

Talk to Others

I don't just mean others on a magical path, although of course this is very useful when you need guidance with spells, ritual, and meditation; there will always be others who have more experience than you, and they will get just as much out of sharing their experiences with you as you will. Trust me! Also, speak to those who can give you an insight into your ancestry, or into folklore, or superstition. Learn about the place you grew up from others so you can compare your experiences. If you find a place you love, talk to someone there and find out what it's like from a local's point of view. Use the internet. If there's a ritual that you are doing and you feel as if you should be doing it differently, seek guidance. Look at forums, groups, even Facebook. Just don't take everything you hear or read as gospel. There is no right or wrong with witchcraft. If you find someone who is telling you their way is the only way and you are wrong if you don't follow it, back away.

Be Outdoors

If you are able, get outside as much as possible. I feel a terrible hypocrite as I write these words, as I have been sat with my computer for around six hours today, wasting a bright albeit blustery day making my eyes and fingers sore. But tomorrow I will be out and about with my little boy, and the week after I am going camping with friends, and the week after that I am camping again for the Summer Solstice. As a witch you are connected to the land you walk upon, and going outside into the world, feeling that land under your feet; it recharges your batteries and gives you perspective. Your home is (or should be) your nest. It is everything about you (and your family/house-mates if you have them) and it should surround and nourish you. But without stepping away from this cocoon of self, you cannot really appreciate it. Moving through the outside world gives us context. It allows us to see ourselves as a part of the world; a cog in the never-ending machinations of the universe, small but crucial.

The other benefit to being outside is learning about the world outside our own routine. Away from jobs and cars and school runs and deadlines and cooking and tidying and bedtime; away from all this is where we expand our consciousness and knowledge by observing the turning of the world. Just now I paused, cocked my head and listened to Lon Dubh (the blackbird) telling me dusk is approaching. He's speaking to the other birds, not me, but his voice touches something inside me that tingles with fascination and the fantasy that I could go outside and sing to him too. It doesn't matter that this is illogical; the bird would not appreciate my song and doubtless neither would the neighbours! But it is a pleasant thought that would not have occurred had I not had the back door open to let his gentle but persistent music in. Nature is inspiration, and inspiration is the root of the ever growing tree of magic.

Look for the Aes Sídhe

The signs are everywhere, in white feathers that fall from the sky; one black swan swimming among the white; an animal that appears everywhere you go; a song that suddenly sounds on every radio you pass. Omens and portents do exist, and it is one skill of the witch to decide which are relevant and which are simply the Sídhe passing by. In *A Modern Celt* I spoke to many people who had experienced the Sídhe or who knew others who had. There were tales of speaking with the dead, visiting with us through the veil that divides our realm from theirs. There were tales of leprechauns or little folk, and even of banshees. Not all experiences with the Sídhe, the Tuatha Dé Danann or the fae (all different names for the Celtic 'fairy folk') are so obvious though. I have felt the Morrígan at my back, great black wings unfolding and pushing me forward with their strength. But these intense experiences are few and far between, and often more terrifying than inspiring. There is no shame in being scared of the fae. They are awesome, and unearthly, and incredibly powerful. Once you move further down the path of a Celtic witch, you accept that these beings are real, and of course this gives them even more power. The key is to be strong willed, firmly believing in the work you do as this will impress those that walk alongside, unseen.

If you want to harness the power of any of these beings, learn about them first. Speak to others who have experience with them. Read appropriate books. For example, if you wanted to learn more about the Morrígan, I would refer you to Morgan Daimler's *The Morrígan: Meeting the Great Queens* or Sorita d'Este's *Guises of the Morrigan*. Learn what the right offerings are, the right places to meet and the right words to say. Then of course, use this knowledge combined with your own experience so you can make up your own mind what the right thing to do is.

Be Cynical and Open-Minded Equally

If someone tells you they speak with Lugh and the Dagda on a daily basis and can teach you how for £500 a month, smile and say, 'No thanks!' politely, but firmly. There are always going to be those who make huge claims with little evidence and try to make big bucks along the way. It's a real shame that the world is full of charlatans and con artists, and you cannot be expected to know, for certain, who is telling the truth at any given time.

However, do not let this knowledge jade you. There are many, many people with deeply spiritual and magical leanings who are often happy to help, to advise, and yes, to sell you education. Be sensible; if something seems too good to be true, the old adage is 'it probably is', but that does not mean we should turn away from every opportunity because there is a chance we could get burned.

Being a witch will bring you into contact with many types of people. Some of these may become friends for life if you remain open to the possibility. Just be prepared for the strength to cut people out of your life if it seems they are not truly who they purport to be.

Become Part of a Community

This does not need to be your local community. Many of us live in areas where we may never speak to our neighbours, or even see them. But there are many other ways of being part of a community. Once again, there is the internet. If you find a forum with sensible, like-minded people, don't be afraid to ask to join. If you join, and you don't like it or don't get anything out of it, you can always leave again! The same goes for online groups such as Google circles, Facebook groups and the like. Don't be put off by 'trolls', the type who put negative comments on everything and try to make you feel small. Everyone will recognise them for what they are, and if they don't, it may be time to leave that particular group.

Outside the internet, you could look for a local moot or gathering to attend, which should lead you to find out what other events are happening. If there are no Pagan gatherings, have a look for traditional festivals such as Maypole festivals. You will be surprised how many local traditions still have deep Celtic roots. Go along, find out who is in charge, speak to them and offer your services. It's important to be recognised as a useful member of your community, virtual or otherwise. It gives you confidence in yourself, and a sense of pride and accomplishment in helping others. It reinforces the image of the witch as a cornerstone of the community, rather than the loner huddled over a cauldron. Just to be clear though, I often am a loner huddled over a cauldron (well, a big pan anyway), I just don't want everyone to know it!

For me, several things help take me outside the house and my own ruminations. I help out at a kitchen for the homeless once a month, and help spread the word about pay-as-you-feel services in Leeds for those who struggle to afford food. I also sing and perform poetry live, taking my creativity into live spaces for others to enjoy. It's not about being important. It's more about doing important things; things that matter to someone else. My friend cares for two elderly people whose families have, sadly, abandoned them. She thinks nothing of it, but to those two old ladies, she is a superhero. It's these small (or large) acts of kindness that help define our character, and it is this behaviour that makes us part of a community.

Embrace Light and Darkness Equally

As a witch you have to accept that you have the potential to do bad things; to be 'evil', for want of a better word. The terms 'good' and 'bad' are subjective, so please, think of them in terms of your own, personal values. Most people go through their daily lives with a general sense of 'being good', firmly believing they are incapable of theft, vandalism or murder. A witch has to accept that she is a complete human being; the full, flawed package! You are capable of these things, saddening though that may be to those with a sensitive disposition. It is the fact that you choose not to do these 'wrong' things that gives you your power.

To perform magic, you must accept the truth that you are capable of anything. This, unfortunately, includes all the nasty things we would rather not think about. Kicking puppies, that sort of thing. However, because you examine these thoughts and choose not to behave in this way, you give yourself enormous power. You take all the potential of those horrible actions and focus all that energy into the things you want to do. Which I really, really hope is not kicking puppies. You have to let the darkness in, before you can expel it, or at least dismiss it.

This may not make sense to those of you who believe all witches are good, or have been taught that positive thinking is the key to everything. Let me clear it up in one sentence: There is no such thing as a white witch. Witches are grey, if any colour at all.

In the words of J. Michael Straczynski:

We stand between the candle and the star.
We stand between the darkness and the light.

These lines have always resonated with me, as they are the perfect representation of the line you have to walk as a witch. You will always be on the edge of things; in the liminal spaces and times. You will guard the veil at the times it opens and closes. You will care for the sick and maybe even watch over the dying. You will be entrusted with great secrets you cannot yet even fathom. You will learn mysteries beyond our most learned scientists that somehow seem simple to you. You will surpass your mentors and be astonished by your descendants, of blood or otherwise. You will learn the language of at least one other living creature and constantly be baffled by another. You will walk on mud, silt, fields, sand, moss, rocks, riverbeds, and sometimes over broken glass or coals. You will hurt and you will see others hurt, but you will feel the mightiest of joys when you ease the pain of a loved one or pull them from their funk.

You will walk with awesome beings from a time completely unlike our own yet a world that is exactly the same. You will be separated from the supernatural by the thinnest of veils that, with focus, you can pull back and peep behind. You will be scared, but you will keep moving forward. You will stumble and you will get up again. You will find forks in your path and not know which way to go, so you will simply choose and move forward, and feel no shame if in time you return to the same fork again.

You will read, you will run, you will cook; you will watch the moon and the sun, you will smell the warm, sweet breath of summer and marvel at the difference between that and the cold, sharp tang of winter. You will marvel equally at the snow that never melts on a mountaintop and the fragility of a caterpillar's cocoon. You will cast spells and some will work and some won't, but you will write it all down, figure out what went wrong and keep trying because that's what a witch does. You will be in a constant state of flux: learning, testing, resting and starting all over again.

Does this frighten you? Or does it excite you? It excites me still, and I have been doing this for some time now. I hope, beyond anything else, that you will re-read all the chapters that resonated with you, and that the next thing you do is put the book down, go out into the world and find where your next stepping stone is.

Cross that great river with my blessing. Craft the ford, navigate the swirls and eddies and never, ever feel you have learned enough. See the magic in everything, and everything you do will be magical.

One final triad:

Three maidens that bring love to good fortune: silence, diligence, sincerity.

Be silent that you may hear; be diligent that you may learn; be sincere that you may always be trusted and respected. Slán agus beannacht leat.

Moon Books invites you to begin or deepen your encounter with Paganism, in all its rich, creative, flourishing forms.